'How to Protect and Grow Your Wealth'

WARNING: The U.S. Dollar and Economy are failing! SMART INVESTORS are Buying Hard Assets (precious metals, farm land, residential real estate, etc.) which never fall to zero. International Assets should be in strong foreign currencies and physical assets, all owned by a foreign trust, to safely increase value, minimize taxes, and avoid capital controls and confiscation by the US government!

Author: David Redick

Acknowledgements: The author gratefully acknowledges permission to reprint excerpts from leading authors and thinkers, plus text and data from web sites. All are noted herein and are presented within the'Fair Use' laws.

Disclaimer: This book is for educational purposes and should not be construed as investment, tax, or legal advice. All statements in this book should be checked and verified by the Reader. This book may contain technical or other inaccuracies, omissions, or typos for which the author has no responsibility. Consult with a licensed professional.

Edition	Date	Pages
First	April, 2014	106
Current, 2M	August, 2018	110

Published by: 'Forward USA Foundation'.

Library of Congress Book Codes:
ISBN-13: 978-1497416567
ISBN-10: 1497416566

Printed in the USA by CreateSpace (Createspace.com), a DBA of On-Demand Publishing LLC, part of the Amazon group of companies.

This book is available at book stores and popular on-line book sellers such as Amazon.com for US$ 12, plus tax and freight.
See Dave's other books there also.

Dedication

This book is written for, and dedicated to, investors who are aware of, and concerned about, the risk of economic decline in the USA, and the falling purchasing power of the U.S. Dollar (not its' exchange value against other failing currencies). You are willing to look beyond the limited asset diversification recommendations issued by 'traditional', 'conventional', or 'mainstream' bankers, brokers, and financial advisors (usually all in U.S. dollars), and consider the added diversification of focusing on hard assets (land, precious metals. residential real estate, etc.), 'Internationalization' by converting most of your assets into safer foreign currencies, trust arrangements, and under the jurisdiction of a nation with a record of stable 'business-friendly' laws and property rights. The book gives you ideas on how to do it. It provides education, not advice.

The expected benefits are lower taxes through trusts, few or no capital controls, low risk of confiscation, multi-generational succession, and worldwide investment choices.

I hope this book helps you protect and grow your wealth.

Wise Thoughts from Leading Investors….

"A country that attracts investment from abroad through stable and fair governance, low taxes, a growing economy, and a productive labor force, and produces goods that are in demand globally will generally see a rising currency value. Strong currencies encourage savings, keep real interest rates low, lower capital costs, and allow for greater productivity and higher real wages." **Peter Schiff**, CFA, CEO, Europac.net, Schiff.gold.org.

"We believe that free markets look after themselves, and that the more free markets are influenced by government intervention, changes in supply and demand, or shifting public psychology, the more an otherwise healthy market gets distorted. The unintended consequences of these market dislocations can be painfully negative for the unaware, but they can be very profitable for those who take early advantage of the investing opportunities they offer." **Doug Casey**, Chairman, CaseyResearch.com

"Throughout history, investors have turned to gold as a store of value in times of turmoil to protect their wealth from the inflation caused by declining paper currency values." , **Brett K. Rentmeester**, CFA, Pres., WindrockWealth.com

"If there has been a more dangerous time for your wealth in human history we are unaware of it. Never before has there been such risk to assets across the entire globe. What happens when the US dollar, the world's primary reserve currency, and all other fiat currencies collapse. **Jeff Berwick**, CEO, (dollarvigilante.com, tdvoffshore.com, tdvwealthmanagement.com, tdvpassports.com, tdvmedia.com)

Part 1:
Chapters   **Page**

(see Part 2 on next page)

Part 2: General Appendix

List of Tables and Figures

****

Part 1:

Introduction

Key Issues

Chapters 1 to 3 explain how the USA money, banking, and securities systems started and works today, and how the abuse of these systems by politicians, 'banksters', and other 'interest groups' has caused the decline in strength of our money and economy. Over 95% of Americans living today have never experienced a depression, or severe recession. Except for the 'bubble burst' losses in 2008, which has been temporarily repaired by massive increases in our money supply ('monetary inflation') called 'Quantitative Easing' by the Federal Reserve System ('Fed', the U.S. central bank) all stock, bonds, and real estate investments have increased in price since their teen years, and most people expect it to continue. Americans tend to look at losses as minor 'corrections' or 'bumps' in the upward path. Well folks, the bad times are here, and investors need to 'wake up' and become aware that after decades of high spending and borrowing, the USA economy is now approaching the cliff of a crash in US Dollar value (over 50% loss), major investment losses, and consumer price increases (hyperinflation). In Chapter 4, I give you ideas on how to protect and grow your wealth during these perilous times. I suggest that you start this book by reading the Glossary to avoid misunderstandings.

Condition of the U.S. Economy

We need major changes in fiscal and monetary policy to help end distortions and losses in the USA economy, and to end how the endless fake money funds, wars, and corruption in government and the financial services industry. Most people now view the government as the source of laws and funding to 'fix' anything, and the

Constitution is ignored as 'old fashioned'. The Federal government gets the most attention because, with its compliant Federal Reserve System (Fed), it can create new money at will. Of course, once the door is opened a bit for the government to 'help' and 'manage' social and business projects, it is pushed wide open by those seeking personal and legal favors! The economic and moral decline of our country, and our worldwide Empire-USA, are the result.

What does our monetary system have to do with this? The key underlying issues are: 1. Internationally, the U.S. dollar is the world's primary reserve currency (treated 'good as gold' for bank reserves, and used in 70% of international transactions, even when the U.S. is not a party; it was 70% before 2008), thus we can create dollars out of thin air to pay our foreign debts (imports and loans) with our own currency (most nations must buy US Dollars) without facing exchange rates (very handy for our big spending government !), and 2. Our central bank, the Federal Reserve System, creates new fake money to fund the excessive federal spending (politicians like that better than raising taxes), plus recent massive bailouts of firms run by their friends, using phony reasons such as 'too big to fail'.

In addition to 'normal' borrowing to fund deficits due to our excessive spending for 'welfare, warfare, and empire', our federal debt increases because, 1. Our foreign suppliers often invest in U.S. Treasury securities with the dollars we pay them for our imports, thus making it easier for us to borrow and spend more, and 2. More borrowing and new money is needed because U.S. states become dependent on federal money as they seek and accept grants, pork, and federally funded state projects with strings attached (happily provided by vote-seeking congresspersons). All of this federal spending leads to an excessive increase in our money supply, which causes price inflation and eventual failure of the US dollar (USD) as its value (purchasing power, not just exchange rate to other failing currencies) drops worldwide. Thus, our mode of operation is unsustainable and must end.

Broadly, a 'monetary system' for a nation is used to create money and control its' use. It includes the currency (physical coins and paper, or their electronic form; see Glossary), mints, various types of private (not government owned) banks, and usually a 'central bank' which manages the system and stores the nation's reserves (gold, currency of other nations, etc.). In most nations, the central bank is openly owned and operated by the government, but our central bank, the 'Federal Reserve System' is a so-called 'private' corporation which includes 12 regional Federal Reserve Banks which carry out much of the System's day-to-day operations. A seven-member Board of Governors in Washington, D.C. is an independent government agency charged with overseeing the Federal Reserve System. The **Board members are appointed by the President and confirmed by the Senate**, and thus are inevitably subject to pressure from politicians. So much for independence from politics!

As with developed nations today, we control our monetary system tightly, including 'legal tender' laws that in various ways force people to use the 'official' government money. History shows us that private money (issued by non-government mints) and banking always works well, where anyone can create 'commodity' money such as gold coins valued by weight of 24 ct gold. Paper notes can be issued for convenience in handling but must be redeemable for gold by the issuing firm to any bearer on demand. Anyone can start and run a bank or mint (license optional), and the only government role is to prevent fraud and theft (see 'Private Gold Standard' on page 104). The crooks that create and push fake money (as in dope 'pushers') are soon discovered and no one will use their money or bank.

However, when the government is the crook, and uses legal tender laws to force use of their fake 'fiat' money (not redeemable for gold; we call ours 'Federal Reserve Notes'), it is harder for the citizens to make corrections! Politicians always try to gain control of the system so they can manipulate it to fund projects that will enhance their jobs, egos, and power. They make new fiat money out of thin air, debase coins (reduce precious metal content or coin size), etc. 'Fiat' means the government declares the 'face value' of metal or paper money without regard to the market-based value of the material of which it is made. They also borrow money from banks and other nations, usually by selling bonds. Bankers have the same incentive to control government (with loans, bribes and threats), and thus the monetary system, and history shows they have been successful at it. Their favorite method is to control the central bank of a nation, and it is said they arrange 'troubles' (wars, assassinations) for those who won't cooperate. The Rothschild banking family has been preeminent worldwide in starting and controlling central banks. The formative days of banking and securities dealers in the U.S. (through 1930) were dominated by the families of Morgan, Rockefeller, Warburg, Carnegie, Harriman, du Pont, Astor, and Kennedy. Their legacy of government control is still with us.

The world has a long history of nations that have failed due to abuse of their monetary system to fund wars, excessive spending, and corruption. The failed empires (they had lots of colonies) of Rome, France, Portugal, Spain and England are examples. Sadly, the USA is in the late stage of a failing empire for the same reasons. We don't have colonies (occupy and control another nation), but with our over 800 bases in 130 countries (and growing), we exert a lot of control, which has the same effect. **The bureaucrats and parasites that run failing governments get**

desperate to save their power and that accounts for most of the illegal and abusive conduct discussed in this book!

Given those historical trends, where are we today? It is not surprising that our monetary system, and those in most of the world, are controlled by corrupt politicians, securities dealers (aka 'Wall Street'), and bankers. Learned economists join the group-thought to have secure jobs. The greed and treachery of these financial industry leaders and their willing dupes caused the world depression and price-monetary inflation that started in 2007 and is still dragging on a bit as I write in Jan-2018. Greed is a human trait and present wherever humans operate, and in any type of political or economic system. When self-serving people get control of a government, and a country's financial system, major distortions, wars, and then economic and moral failure, always occur.

In summary, if the above issues seem important to you, read this book and then start selection of a Wealth Manager to create your plan for more wealth, and less risk and taxation. I wish you Good and Safer Investing!

Please send comments to Redickd@aol.com.
To see my essays on various topics, go to ActivistPost.com, select 'Contributors' at top of the Home page, then scroll down to my name.
Note that some of my articles are also shown on P. 89 to 97 below

Thanks for your interest, Dave Redick

****

Chapter 1: The US Monetary System

Why Do We Have Money

Let's discuss the concept of money, why it is needed, and some definitions. Barter (exchange cloth for some apples, etc.) can work, but is cumbersome and full of problems. The cloth seller might not want apples, or your variety, and apples rot in storage, etc., so the concept of an intermediary 'medium of exchange' (called 'money') was invented (by people, not the government) as a 'general purpose' means to buy anything. Any seller will accept it if, 1) he thinks it will hold its' value, and 2) he can use it to buy from others – ie., sellers will accept it. Various commodities (the same worldwide; by grade and type) such as metals, shells, hoes, and tobacco, etc., which have market value when not used as money, have been used as money, and all served the need for;

1) a medium of exchange,

2) a unit of account. For pricing, use weight - gram, etc.-of the commodity; don't use a 'name' like 'Dollar' which allows change/reduction by the issuer of the weight it represents, and

3) a store (savings) and measure of value (when compared to other things).

On this basis, gold always emerges as best (silver, nickel, copper and zinc follow), due to its' 'characteristics, shown on p. 64. **Note that the value of the transaction equals the market value of the commodity used in the coins**.

A KEY POINT is that the amount of commodity material the money is made of is equal in market value to the good or service being purchased! I have not seen this point mentioned in any of my reading. I presume it is missing due to lack of awareness, Others disagree with me, or want to retain 'flexibility' in abusing a monetary system for the benefit of the issuer. Money's 'value' (or 'purchasing power'; 'PP') is set by scarcity and demand of the goods, services, and/or gold available in a market area (nation, region). The gold price should not be set by government 'management' as recommended by Steve Forbes, and Ames, in their 2014 book 'Money'. Further, he only wants a 'link' to gold, not my plan where '**gold is money, with weight of 24 ct in the coin as the unit of account'.** Forbes' approach is doomed to self-serving manipulation by the government. Since Forbes is a 'big-government conservative', this approach is not surprising. Money 'stability' is his main goal', not market value and PP. Shame on Cato.org leaders for praising the book. They also like Milton Friedmans' 'management' of the money supply by the Fed. Bad thinking for a so-called free-market org.

Free-market, not biased by politics, setting of the PP of gold is basically a roving auction process where people shop-around for the best price and quality, then buy it with a weight of gold they agree on with the seller, thus setting the PP. Sellers who find they are losing business to competitors must prove their product is 'worth it' (by advertising, demos) or cut their price. This is called 'market clearing', or 'equilibrium', where no external forces (government intervention, fraud, monopoly, etc.) affect the buyers' choices. This process is self-regulating and needs no government control. The millions of transactions for all types of things (good, services, land interest, stock, etc.) all contribute to setting the PP of gold in a market area. Yes, there can be differences between 'areas' but this prompts transaction activity between areas (regions, nations; in the absence of damaging government meddling 'mercantilism' import tariffs and controls) that tends to make PP close to equal in all areas. Yeah for free-market pricing for good, services, and money!!

Gold is heavy, and wears-away with handling (weight/value loss) and, so paper 'notes' were invented as a convenience in handling and storage. At first the notes were just a 'claim check' on gold coins (the gold is the 'money; not just 'backing') held by the issuer (mint, bank, etc.) of the notes, and redeemable for gold coin by any bearer on demand. The issuers soon realized they could create more notes than they could redeem, and 'fractional reserve' minting started (then the banks used FR deposits to do more and bigger loans). All governments noticed this and soon began laws (legal tender, mint licenses, taxes, and restrictions) to make themselves the sole issuer (a monopoly) in their area of control (nation, colonies, etc.) so they could create more money than they could redeem (politically better than taxing). The U.S. has been doing this since 1971 when Nixon abrogated the Bretton Woods agreement (made us redeem dollars to other nations for $35 per oz. of gold).

A Brief History of Money

Metal objects were introduced as money around 5,000 B.C. By 600 BC, the Lydians (now part of Turkey) became the first in the Western world to make precious metal coins of a certain weight, fineness (purity), and shape. Their **Stater** was made of electrum, a naturally occurring mixture of gold and silver. The Roman **Denarius** was a small silver coin first minted about 211 BC. The Arabs used the gold **Dinar**, which still in use. Its' name evolved from the Denarius, as did the Spanish word for money; 'dinero'. Greece used the silver **Drachma**. The Byzantine **Solidus** (meaning 'solid') **gold** coin, which evolved to the **Bezant**, was introduced by Emperor Constantine I, in 312 AD, permanently replacing the **Aureus** as the gold coin of the Roman Empire. The Bezant was about 4.5 grams of 23 ct gold, and was maintained essentially unaltered in weight, dimensions and purity for 600 years. This stability of value was a key factor in the prosperity of those times. For more on old coins, see; http://en.wikipedia.org/wiki/List_of_historical_currencies.

Some of the earliest known paper money (not redeemable for metal) was about AD 960 in China. Since this money was made of material with little or no market value when not used as money, it was often abused by over-production and became worthless. The world's first central bank was the Bank of England, founded in 1694. It was a privately owned bank, but was given special privileges by the King, such as buying royal bonds with their paper notes. At first, the notes were redeemable in specie (gold or silver), but excessive creation of 'notes' soon started, redeemability ended, and their value dropped. In 1699 King William III appointed physicist Sir Isaac Newton as Master of the Mint to develop rules for management of the banks' money. Newton developed what we now call the "Classical Gold Standard' with paper notes, or base-metal token coins, redeemable in a certain weight and purity of gold at the issuing bank or mint, by bearer on demand. The rules started in 1707, but were soon broken and price inflation followed. The British Pound still survived as a 'good as gold' coin and the world's reserve currency until 1914 when they suspended gold redemption so they could inflate the money supply to pay for WW1. The Bank of England was nationalized into a central bank in 1946

In the USA

The American colonies created 'colonial scrip' (paper currency not redeemable for a commodity such as gold). It worked well for a few years but it was abused by excessive expansion of supply (monetary inflation) in some areas, and became worthless. This gave our Founders fair warning about the problems with paper money. The King of England frowned on their attempts at monetary independence and their scrip was banned by English Parliament in the 'Currency Act of 1764'. This caused a depression in the colonies, and was one of the reasons for the American Revolution. Notice that this is not in the government-approved history books in our schools!

The Colonies, and early US states, used many types of currency from other nations, and had no 'official' U.S. money. The 'Spanish Milled Dollar' (or '8 Reales') was prominent due its known silver content (averaged 27.47 grams of 0.93 fine silver, but varied with mint and date; Wiki). People often cut these coins into pie-slice shaped halves, quarters, and eighths (or 'bits') to make change. This was the origin of "pieces of eight", and '2 bits' equals a quarter dollar.

Following Alexander Hamilton's recommendations to create a national currency, Congress enacted the 'Coinage Act of 1792' (The Mint Act). It established gold and silver as the monetary standards of the United States with the gold set at 15 times the value of silver. This fixed 'bi-metallic' standard caused trouble later! The initial US silver dollar coins were struck of 26.96 grams of 0.8924 fine silver (alloyed with copper). The diameter was 39 to 40 millimeters with a lettered edge reading 'HUNDRED CENTS ONE DOLLAR OR UNIT'. The act also allowed for the creation of a national mint. It was the world's first decimal-based monetary system.
Between the adoption of the Constitution and the Civil War the United States government did not issue paper money as we know it today, but on many occasions it did issue short term debt called Treasury Notes. They also issued Demand Notes that were intended to function as money, and were authorized within the legal framework of Treasury Notes. This was a 'sneaky' ploy since the U.S. was not generally assumed to have the authority to issue banknotes at that time.

The Continental Congress had issued Continental dollars between 1775 and 1779 to help finance the American Revolution. The paper Continental dollars nominally entitled the bearer to an equivalent amount of Spanish

19

Milled dollars but were never redeemed in silver and lost 99% of their value by 1790 despite the American victory. Some claim that British General Howe printed thousands of Continentals and sold them cheaply in order to destroy its value. With the fate of the Continentals in mind, the Founding Fathers put no provision for a paper currency in the Constitution. Article 1, Sec 10 says the states may use only gold or silver coin as legal tender. As a result, the pre-Civil War circulation of banknotes in the United States consisted of private issues, including issues by private federally chartered banks such as the First and Second banks of the U.S. (more below). The Coinage Act of 1834 set gold at 16 times the value of silver, which undervalued the silver, causing traders to export it for use abroad.

In 1861 Lincoln needed money to finance the so-called 'Civil War' (actually a war of aggression against the South, which had the right to secede, to retain them as a source of cotton, and a market for Northern manufactured goods), so he went with his Secretary of the Treasury to New York to apply for the necessary loans. The Bankers (money changers), wishing the Union forces to fail, offered loans at annual rate of 24% to 36%. Lincoln declined the offer. An old friend of Lincoln's, Colonel Dick Taylor of Chicago, was put in charge of solving the problem of how to finance the war. His solution is recorded as this: "Just get Congress to pass a bill authorizing the printing of full legal tender treasury notes... and pay your soldiers with them and go ahead and win your war with them also." The initial 'Greenbacks' were redeemable in gold or silver, but redemption soon ended so the Legal Tender Act of 1862 was issued to force people and firms to accept them. Next came the National Bank Acts of 1863 and 1864 that created a system of federally chartered 'national' banks that issued bank notes supplied by the new 'Office of the Comptroller of the Currency' (OCC) and US Mint (both part of the Department of the Treasury). The Acts also put a ten

20

percent tax on state-issued bank notes, which ended their money-making profit (as planned by DC) so they all quit, **which gave us a federal monopoly on money creation!** These Acts, and creation of the DC-controlled Fed in 1913, were the start of excessive paper 'money' creation ('monetary inflation') that caused the Great Depression of the 1930s, then various recessions, and peaked in the huge 2008 crash, with the worse yet to come!

U. S. Silver Coins and Certificates

The next major banking law was the 'Fourth Coinage Act of 1873' led by Pres. Grant that demonetised silver and effectively put the US on the gold standard, which replaced the gold and silver bimetallic standard that had been created by Alexander Hamilton. Many of the poorer citizens saw this as a "crime," which prompted passage of the Bland-Allison Act by Congress on February 28, 1878. It did not provide for the "free and unlimited coinage of silver" demanded by Western miners, but it did require the United States Treasury to purchase between $2 million and $4 million of silver bullion from mining companies in the West, to be minted into coins that would be legal tender for all debts, like gold. Paper 'Silver Certificate' money was first issued in 1878 and bore the words; 'Silver Certificate, This certifies that there is on deposit in the Treasury of the United States of America 'x' Dollars in silver payable to the Bearer on Demand', and 'This Certificate is Legal Tender for all Debts, Public and Private.' Most were $1, $2, and $5. Redemptions were paid in $1 silver coins.

The Gold Standard Act of 1900 ended bi-metalism (use of both gold and silver coins for note redemption), set 1.5046 grams of pure 24k gold per dollar (thus $20.67 per troy ounce; 31.1 gr per troy oz./1.5046), and required the US Mint to hold enough gold to redeem at least 40% of certificates issued (a fractional reserve).

Next, the bankers conspired to get the Federal Reserve System approved on December 23, 1913 (more on P. 22). Today's 'Federal Reserve Notes' only bear the words 'This Note is Legal Tender for all Debts Public and Private'. JFK was planning to bypass the Fed by having the Treasury issue 'U.S. Notes' (certificates redeemable in silver) and silver coins. Some say this partly led to his assassination.

The original Act required 35 and 40% (large or small banks) gold reserves for dollar notes issued, but by 1962, that had been reduced to 12%, using of Fed Notes as reserves!

The Morgan silver dollar coin (1878-1921), and the Peace (1921-1935) had 0.8 oz. of 0.9 purity, thus 0.72 oz.; four quarters or ten dimes had the same total, and all had wide usage. Pres. Johnson approved the 'Coinage Act of 1965' which ended silver content in coins (their bullion market value had exceeded their face value), thus 1964 and prior coins (known as 'junk' silver due to wear) were 'hoarded' and valued for their silver content. Now the quarter is 91.67 percent copper and 8.33 percent nickel. Pennies are 97.5% zinc and 2.5% copper. The exception was the Kennedy half dollar which started in 1964 as a memorial (he died on Nov. 22, 1963) with 90% silver (0.362 oz), then 40% in 1965-70 and zero after1971. The Eisenhower silver dollar in 1971-78 had 0.316 oz. Redemption of Silver Certificates for metal ended in Oct-1967, but they remain legal tender. Nixon abrogated the Bretton Woods Agreement in August, 1971, which required redemption of paper notes with gold at $35 oz. We were running out of gold due to redemptions prompted by our lavish money creation and spending the 1960s. This ended all US Dollar ties to precious metal.

The Petrodollar System ; A likely crash of the 1971 floating, goldless, USD (US Dollar) was saved by the **Petrodollar System, a paper crutch!**. The deal is

explained in this excerpt from a Jan-2012 article by Marin Katusa of www.CaseyResearch.com; *"To explain this situation properly, we have to start in 1973. That's when President Nixon asked King Faisal of Saudi Arabia to accept only US dollars as payment for oil and to invest any excess profits in US Treasury bonds, notes, and bills. In exchange, Nixon pledged to protect Saudi Arabian oil fields from the Soviet Union and other interested nations, such as Iran and Iraq..."*

By 1975 all of the members of OPEC agreed to sell their oil only in US dollars. Every oil-importing nation in the world started saving their surplus in US dollars so as to be able to buy oil; with such high demand for dollars the currency strengthened. On top of that, many oil-exporting nations like Saudi Arabia spent their US dollar surpluses on Treasury securities, providing a new, deep pool of lenders to support US government spending." For the entire article, visit: http://www.caseyresearch.com/cdd/demise-petrodollar.

Notice that the Oil Embargo, related to the Yom Kippur War, started in 1974. OPEC demanded, and got, price increases to $12.20 bbl in 1975 and $25 by 1979 (but this only accounted for inflation since the $2.77 price in 1948; it had been only $3.50 in 1973!!). The Petrodollar system continues today, but is weaker as a support of the USD value due to major transactions between oil producers (including Russia), and big buyers like China, India, and others, dealing in their own currencies. In 2017 China opened Yuan bond sales in 9 countries. It also introduced the 'Yuan-Dollar', which is redeemable for gold! The battle is joined!!

The big drop in crude prices from $ 115 per barrel in early 2014 to $50 (and falling) through 2015 are mostly due to; 1) the U.S. trying to hurt Russia (less income from oil exports), and 2) major production and exports from the U.S. due to fracking. The price drop has bankrupted many U.S. 'frackers', and many gulf off-shore rigs have closed.

The reasons the US invaded Iraq and Libya (and is threatening Iran) were; 1) Their leaders had started selling oil for gold and other currencies; a death warrant! , and 2) Getting their oil and denying it to China. Based on recent large gold purchases, maybe China and Russia are planning to destroy the petrodollar system by using gold as money (or 'backing' for the ruble and yuan), and thus crash the U.S. economy by ending the USD's role as the world's primary reserve currency (see more on the IMF SDR on p. 42, and the Petro-Yuan on p. 56). During the March, 2014 exchanges of threats concerning the Ukraine, Russian Pres. Putin mentioned ending use of the USD. His plan got stronger after his May 21, 2014 $400 bill. oil deal with China, using their own currencies! His threat is credible, and reveals the weakness of the USD and Empire-USA ! See more on p.48.

Abuse of their monetary system is done by most governments. See Table 4 on p-77 for the current rankings. of strength. This order has been similar for hundreds of years. One popular form of abuse is for the issue more paper notes than they can redeem with gold (fractional reserve; issuer of the primary reserve currency does it the most), until Sellers and bond buyers finally refuse to use it, and it crashes in value. Then Sellers choose a better currency, as shown in Table 7. All signs indicate the USD will lose it's status soon (10-30 years?).

Table 7: Years a Country Issued Reserve Currency

Country	Start	End	Years	Coin
Roman Empire	200 BC	300	100	Aureus
Byzantine Emp.	300	1100	800	Solidus , Bezant
Florence	1200	1450	250	Fiorino
Portugal	1450	1525	75	Escador, Real
Spain	1525	1635	110	Real de la Ocho
Netherlands	1635	1710	75	Guilder
France	1710	1815	105	Franc
UK-Britain	1815	1925	110	Pound Sterling
USA	1925	Now	93 +	US Dollar

(Source- www.Engcoms.com)

Use of the coins from the first 3 nations was regional, the last 6 were worldwide. The Byzantine Empire was a spin-off from Rome, and based in Constantinople. It's gold Solidus coin evolved to the Bezant. They kept their full gold content over the years, which accounts for their long usage, and the prosperity of the region. The Aureus failed due to debasement by Rome. See p-17.

Early USA Central Banks:

Politicians like central banks that control the national monetary system because they can manipulate them to gain funding by creating new money, without politically unpopular taxation. In 1791, the 'First Bank of the United States', (BUS-1), was started, but it failed in 1811. The second attempt was the 'Second Bank of the U. S.' (BUS-2), chartered in 1816, with a renewal required in 1836.

"The main reason the Second Bank of the United States was chartered was that in the War of 1812, the U.S. experienced severe inflation and had difficulty in financing military operations. Pres. Andrew Jackson strongly

opposed the renewal of the 'second' bank's charter, and won." (wikipedia.org)

Creating the Federal Reserve System

'All central banks are created by and for politicians and bankers, so neither runs out of money'; by Redick, 2014

The Federal Reserve System should be considered the third U.S. central bank (BUS-3). The secret plan to create the financial monster now known as the 'Fed' was consummated on November 22, 1910 at a private club on Jekyll Island, Georgia. Congregated at his clandestine meeting were some of the most powerful political and financial people in Europe and America.

*'The sole intention of these conspirators was to draft a blueprint for a strong central bank that served their interests. Because the Federal Reserve System was to be a bank of issue then, just as the plotters understood all too well, it was **unconstitutional from its inception**.* (www.overlordsofchaos.com)

On Dec. 23, 1913, when many Congresspersons, including major opponents of central banking, had already left town, Congress adopted the Federal Reserve Act, also known as the Owens-Carter Act. Even the name was meant to deceive, so they chose: 1. 'Federal' to make it seem to be part of the government, and 2. 'System' instead of 'Bank' because many Congresspersons opposed a federal bank. They planned the 'system' with twelve regional banks (each a privately owned corporation) to satisfy private bankers that their regional concerns would be heard.

Fake 'Mandates' and the 'Real Reasons' the Fed was Created

A further fake 'selling point' to gain support from the people and Congress was to declare that the 'dual mandate' of the Fed was to maintain; 1. Stable value of the Dollar, and 2. High employment, and the Fed has failed at both! **These fake mandates shielded the 'real' reasons of;**

1. A 'flexible' source of new money for politicians to spend (causing price inflation, a hidden tax), and 2. The 'lender of last resort' role to bail out banks and other firms with good political connections!

This, and other government meddling, led to the 'casino banking' that caused the 2008 crash, with more to come in 2018 and up.

Structure of the Fed

The Federal Reserve System consists of the Board of Governors, the 12 Federal Reserve banks, the Federal Open Market Committee, the Federal Advisory Council, and, since 1976, the Consumer Advisory Council.

The US President appoints the seven members of the Board and they serve for 14 years This makes a joke of 'independence form the government!'
The chairman and vice-chairman are chosen by the President from among the sitting Governors for four-year terms. Thus political independence is a joke! There are also within the system several thousand member banks. The Board of Governors of the Federal Reserve System determines the reserve requirements of the member banks, reviews and determines the discount rates established by the 12 Federal Reserve banks, and reviews their budgets.

Each Federal Reserve Bank is a privately owned corporation established pursuant to the Federal Reserve

Act of 1913 to supposedly serve the public interest. A board of nine directors governs each Federal Reserve Bank, six of whom are appointed by the member banks and three of who are appointed by the Board of Governors of the Federal Reserve System. The 12 Federal Reserve banks are located in Boston, New York, Philadelphia, Chicago, San Francisco, Cleveland, Richmond, Atlanta, St. Louis, Minneapolis, Kansas City and Dallas.

Notice that the word 'reserve' is used extensively above, both in the name of the Fed, and its activities. This is because if a private bank gets low on reserves (compared to the legal requirements at the time), it can't make new loans, and this could be widespread in bad economic times. While a new bank depends on investments by shareholders for its initial reserves, profits and borrowing from the Fed become major sources as it grows. Hence, the Fed's role in loaning banks money to boost their reserves is a powerful tool in 'managing' the level of economic activity nationwide. It also allows the Fed, as 'lender of last resort', to do bail-outs in bad times!

The above description shows how the so-called 'privately owned' Fed bank controls the US monetary system. Not mentioned, is that most of its meetings and actions are secret, even to Congress, and that it is heavily politicized and controlled by the Federal government. It was annoying to see the liar Bernanke plead that Rep. Ron Paul's bill HR-1207 (paul.house.gov; retired Jan-2013) to audit the Fed would reduce its independence. What a joke! He really wants the right to secrecy to help his 'friends'!

But take heart! It's never too late to abolish the Fed and return to the proven gold standard. Since Congress is not likely to support ending their cash cow, the change may originate from another country. **See pages 53 to 57 on the pressure China, Russia, and others, are creating to bring down the USD!**

Chapter 2: Effects of the Fed and Other Central Banks

The Impact of Fake Money

You won't read the following analysis in the newspapers or in a college economics course. Most government and industry leaders and professors like the present system because their jobs, grants, and social life depend on having and supporting it! They want to be viewed as 'normal', not a radical 'gold bug' who likes sound, or 'real', money which means gold or silver coins, and paper notes redeemable in gold by any bearer, on demand. Ignoring precious metals requires a self-serving mental and ethical lapse where the fake nature of the fiat money is ignored.

The creation of fiat 'official' government money has had a profound effect in history and on our nation and the world today. 'Fiat' means it is worth whatever the government says it is (its 'face value'), although the material of which it is made may have more or less market value. Examples are: 1) valuable silver dollars and worthless paper, both declared worth $1, and 2) todays' 'American Eagle' bullion coin with a 'face value' of $50 for one ounce of gold!

KEY POINT ! Normally, when a nation creates too much fake money, sellers avoid it for payment, or stop buying its bonds, due to the falling value of both, and the party is soon over. However, the **US is in a unique position never seen in the history of the world**. Our fiat paper money is the primary de facto (not 'formal', since 1971) world's 'reserve currency' (1. anyone will accept it for payment, and keep it as cash, or as a dollar-denominated asset; 2. over 60% of world transactions use it, thus banks keep large reserves of it). Thus, we can create new money (paper or electronic) out of thin-air by the billions and sellers of goods and services worldwide (and in the U.S.) will accept it, and we can pay our debts with it, even as the federal government spends to excess. **No other country can do that!!** We have abused the 'privileged' status of the U.S. dollar (USD) in many immoral and counterproductive ways. It is the underlying cause (funder) of our major problems with jobs (exported due to excessive imports of goods), banking and securities (strange deals based on loose money), excessive personal spending and debt (borrow, buy and play now, pay later!), and expensive wars.

Table 1
The Honest National Debt and Unfunded Liabilities

A, $ 21.2 tn National Debt (disclosed debt)

B.   112.9   Key Misc. unfunded Liabilities (not disclosed
      27.9   Medicare A, B, and D (unfunded)
      16.9   Social Security (unfunded)

$ 157.7 trillion   Total for B

$ 178.9 trillion = Grand Total (A+B)

(Source: USDebtClock.org, Apr 29, 2018)

The 'official' government debt figures ignore the above Medicare, Soc. Sec. and Misc. items (treated as 'off-budget' !!), plus potential trillions that loom due to $5.3 tn losses at Fannie and Freddie, now government-owned. There are other 'Misc.' items, such as food stamps, not shown above.

The deceit is exposed by the fact that after Congress increased the federal debt limit to $12.104 tn in Feb-2009 (80% of GDP), in Feb-2010 increased it to $14.3 tn, and in

Jan-2012 to $16.4 tn (102% of GDP) which was approached in Dec-2012 stirring the 'fiscal cliff' chaos! On Jan. 23, 2013 they suspended the legal limit on government borrowing until May 19, then agreed on the increase. In Feb., 2014 they agreed to more spending, with no limits, until March, 2015!! In Jan-2017 we face a shutdown of the government due to olack of funding the budget! Government accounting is loaded with hypocrisy. They ignore the normal accounting rules and honesty that apply to mere citizens, in order to hide the problems they have created. They prosecute private firms for doing the same thing! Note that the above figures do not count the trillions for Obama's health plan!

In 1970 the national debt was $380.9 billion (about $3.4 trillion in 2015 dollars), and 37.6% of the GDP. As of Oct.-2015 the national debt was $18.4 tn, and 103% of GDP, and in Jan-2018 $19.9 tn debt and 106.% of GDP, thus reaching the danger level of more debt than GDP!! For definitions of GDP and GNP see p. 100; the government now prefers to use GNP. No one believes the debt will ever be paid. To eliminate it, we can; 1) Increase taxes a lot, 2) Do an overt default (repudiation), and refuse to pay most of it (a serious possibility; Russia and Brazil did!), or 3) Create new fake money (the IMF 'SDR'?), but this would likely cause hyper price inflation, and destroy the US dollar and economy. Horrible choices, all thanks to irresponsible government leaders.

Of course consumer debt (cars, home mortgages – first and second -, credit cards, TVs, student loans, etc.) zoomed upward because of the easy (lax terms, sub-prime), cheap (low interest) fake money created by the Fed from 2000 to 2007. When this bubble burst in 2008, people lost their jobs, bills went unpaid, and defaults and foreclosures followed. Sad.

New fiat money, and lax terms, funded the debt explosion. This excessive credit creates and feeds the abusive and corrupt Wall Street and Main Street excessive spending and debt. One cannot underestimate the importance of our ability to pay our debts to other nations, and not be required to convert to their money. We can simply create new dollars to pay our debts, with only a minor impact on its value in the short-term. Conversely, other nations must buy dollars (or Euros) to pay for most imports or loans, and face declining exchange rates if they have expanded their money supply too much. We have abused this 'reserve' status and in mid-2010 other nations started seeking alternatives (yuan, yen, a 'basket of currencies', etc.). Most people are not aware that the 'reserve' currency is used for most payments between other nations (example: India pays Brazil for coffee with USD). Hence, all nations keep a supply of USD to use in trade. All banks are required to have sufficient 'reserves' to show a strong asset base for the bank's obligations (mainly demand and time deposits). Since the USD has been valued by the world system as 'good as gold', it is known as a 'reserve currency' and used instead of gold to fund these bank reserves. The Dollar was used in about 80% of international transactions since its ascendancy in the 1920's (the English 'Pound Sterling', GBP, faded), but it has become weaker since 2000, and declined to 60% or less in 2015.

About 30% of international deals are now done in a mix of Euros, Swiss francs and Yen, but that is increasing as the economies and currencies of China and others grow stronger. Indeed, China started using its yuan (same as Renminbi, RMB) for international transactions in mid- 2010, and also allowed foreign firms to create a yuan-denominated private equity funds. In 2014, **China lead the world in gold purchases (based on estimates), and together with setting-up yuan-based banking centers worldwide, they will soon be in a position to use the**

32

yuan as a world reserve currency! They could replace the USD, or at least greatly reduce its' dominance, as it fails. (see comments after Table 3)

While 'inflation' of the money supply (like a balloon) reduces the value of every USD, the U.S. government prefers this to deflation because 'free money' from inflation helps pay off federal debts to other nations. In the extreme, this is a form of default, since the lender gets paid in near-worthless paper money. In mid-2010, our lenders (China, etc.) voiced concern about this possibility.

The federal funds target interest rate were at historic lows of about 1% during 2001 to 2005, which was done to stimulate recovery after the 'dot-com' bubble burst on NASDAQ in March-2000. In Jan-2006, Fed Chairman Greenspan increased interest rates to 5.25% to 'put the brakes on', just as he ended his final term and handed the reins (and keys to the vault and printing press?) to Bernanke (and then Ben to Yellen in Feb-2014). The sudden Fed increase caused mortgage rates to rise, which in turn triggered the 2007 decline in housing prices and purchases, and started the worldwide depression. Fed intervention strikes again! The U.S. economy failed quickly because many banks and Wall Street firms were highly leveraged (over 25:1) in risky investments and could not tolerate losses.

During the 2000 to 2007 boom times, Wall Street had been 'securitizing' bundles of various weak and bad debt instruments (subprime mortgages, credit card debt, student loans, etc.) into 'mortgage-backed securities' (MBS), then getting their complicit rating agencies (Moodys, Standard and Poors -S&P-, Fitch) to falsely label them AAA, an act of fraud. By doing so, they could sell them worldwide to get them off their books, and then make more money by making new loans to other weak borrowers.

Massive amounts of cheap fake money, supplied by the Federal Reserve System started and supported these debacles. More money was created for Bush's $700 billion TARP (Troubled Asset Relief Program) in 2008, with the Fed pouring about $2.2 trillion into the economy for their bailouts (the 'Bernanke Spike'), and then $787 bill. more for Obama's Feb-2009 Recovery plan. It's like pouring gas on a fire! This combined $2.987 trillion is now called 'Quantitative Easing-1', or 'QE-1', and showed meager results. Then in Nov-2010 the Fed announced QE-2 to buy $600 billion in long-term U.S. Treasury bonds, ostensibly to push down long-term interest rates, and in Sep-2012 QE-3 to spend $40 bn. per mo. on mortgage-based securities, plus the existing 'Operation Twist' of $45 bn. mo.(to buy and sell short- and long-term US bonds - hence the 'twist - to reduce interest rates), with no end date!

Bernanke specialized in study of the 'Great 1930's Depression' for his Ph.D. program. He claimed that the Fed should have increased the money supply in 1929 when the depression started, instead of reducing it. He was determined to not let that mistake happen again, so in 2008 he bought Treasuries to flood the economy with new money and bought junk assets from banks to save his buddies jobs! The Fed had $800 bn assets in 2008, but grew to $3.7 trill. by Oct-2014!! By then, results had been disappointing as unemployment got worse, and prices rose, so QE was ended. So much for 'fixing by flooding'.

Most of our current economic problems were created by the Fed (with cheering from Congress) by flooding the nation with cheap, fake, money as a stimulant since the early '90s. It should surprise no one that people, bankers, and Wall Street reacted by seeking high-return, risky investments (derivatives, etc.) to help them beat the price inflation caused by this easy money (low interest, lax terms), and excessive expansion of the money supply. A second cause of seeking excessive profits and risk was the 'moral hazard' of knowing they would probably be bailed out by the Fed if they got in trouble. Since its creation in 1913, and with a surge since 2000, the Fed has expanded ('inflated') the money supply by twenty times. 'Price Inflation', a secondary effect caused by inflating the money supply, has reduced the US dollars' (USD) purchasing power by 95% (20:1) since 1913, So much for government management ! Even worse, the Fed now has a 'target' of 2% annual price inflation, claiming that deflation is awful, but in fact it is to give the government more money to spend!

Many people claim that 'unfettered free-market Capitalism' was the cause of the 2008 crash, and call for more regulation. They have re-defined 'capitalism' and 'corporations' so they have straw men to attack.

In fact, **Capitalism is just an 'economic system' based on private ownership, free enterprise, and minimal regulation,** and corporations are primarily just a way to raise money through sale of shares. Capitalism offers more than economic results. **It is a moral system** that depends on the free-market activity of willing buyers and sellers within the rule of law, not coercion and control by others (the government-power folks). A key problem is that we have not had a free market since 1913 (when the Fed was born), and worse since 1933 when FDR declared that the government was our mother and boss, and responsible to provide convenience and security for all, and have 'someone else' (the government or 'the rich') pay for it. **We now have 'crony capitalism'** where the firms and government collude to do favors for each other. The citizens lose! Our nation's culture (honesty, courtesy, personal responsibility, private charity, etc.) and economy (reduced standard of living, higher debt due to more war and welfare, etc.) have been sliding downhill ever since.

Visit my articles f) and g) on p. 90 and 91. Unconstitutional government programs and intervention in the free market have caused most of our problems. This result shows in every country run by central authority in history, and worldwide today.

The Fed's Record of Results

The purchasing power (value) of the US dollar (USD) has dropped by more than 95% (depreciation) since 1913, all due to excessive creation of new money (expansion of the money supply; monetary inflation). This hurts the people (especially those on limited or fixed incomes, and those with savings), but the bankers have done well, since they make money selling US debt (T-bills, etc.) and get bailed-out when in trouble due to their own greed (Bear-Stearns in 2008, etc.). Most Fed meetings are secret, and proceedings are not even available to Congress; Preposterous ! Some economists say the Fed is needed in order to assure adequate 'liquidity' or 'elasticity' for growth by proper expansion of the money supply, equal to growth of the economy; about 3 to 5% per year. The problem is that such powers are **ALWAYS** abused by governments (by expansion of 10 to 20% per year, or more!), though some (the Swiss) less than others (the US is among the worst of the major currencies).
We cannot, and should not, trust the government, or Fed, or any committee or group of people, to 'manage' our monetary system. The chance of bias by politics, corruption and incompetence are too high. Only the market (users of money) 'knows all' and responds without bias. This excessive money causes bad spending and investment decisions at both the business and personal level, which creates financial distortions (big peaks, then valleys), as seen in: 1) Bailing-out England after WW1, leading to mal-investment (too much money around) and the crash of 1929 when, after ten years of excessive

expansion (the 'Roaring 20s'), the money supply was suddenly reduced by about 30% by the Fed, 2) The 2007-2008 housing price and construction collapse due to a Fed interest rate increase of 4.25% (from 1 to 5.25%) in 2006, and 3) Many large peaks and valleys, and 90% loss of USD purchasing value, since the Fed was created. So much for government 'management' of currency and the economy!!

As James Quinn wrote on his web site www.The BurningPlatform.com, in his March 10, 2009 article 'Grand Illusion – The Federal Reserve': *"The average American might just conclude that prices always go up, so what's the big deal about inflation. This is where the Federal Reserve and politicians have pulled the wool over your eyes. The CPI was 30.9 in 1964. Today, it is 211.1. This means that prices have risen 683% since 1964. The only problem is that your wages have not risen at the same rate, even using the government manipulated CPI. Using a true CPI figure, average weekly earnings are 64% below what they were in 1964. This explains why a family of five could live well with one parent working in 1964, but even with both parents working and using debt in prodigious amounts, the average family does not live as well today."*

When nations used real money (precious metal –PM–coins, or tokens and paper certificates -notes- redeemable for PM), they had small highs and lows in their economies, but they were 'self-liquidating' (private investors stop putting limited funds into bad deals), and they never had the huge variations now caused by excessive fake money (investors and the government have lots of money to keep funding lots of deals; good and bad).

The analogy below helps demonstrate what fake money does to an economy, its firms, and people.

The Heroin Analogy

The injection of heroin into your body, or a large increase in the money supply (over 5% per year) into an economy, are both 'stimulants', but cause illness when used to excess. When the stimulants are ended to solve the bad effects, your body suffers from withdrawal, and the economy from recession, or worse! Creating fake money to fund 'stimulus' risks price inflation (reduced purchasing power of the US dollar), but or 'leaders' in DC like it because it is a quick 'fix' (shows that they are 'doing something'), an d also helps them payoff their friends (campaign donors) on Wall Street, and federal debt, with cheap dollars. This is part of the heroin analogy, where our 'leaders' (Obama, Geithner, Bush, Paulson, Bernanke - Fed Chm. since Feb 2006, Yellen since Feb-2014, Greenspan prior, and most Congresspersons) are shameless, dishonest pushers and dealers with their 'bailout' programs. Their priority is to get re-elected (or keep their appointed job) by doing favors for voters, their bosses, and campaign donors, no matter what the long-term harm to the nation and its people!

Global investor Jim Rogers (JimRogers.com) said in Nov-2010; "**The banks who lent the money and made the mistakes should lose money. The bondholders and the stockholders of those banks should lose money**. It's that simple." The logic applies equally in the USA, but campaign donors and pals got bailed-out instead.

As shown in the May 5, 2009 issues of Gary North's Reality Check, Issue 854, www.GaryNorth.com, *"The FED is engaged in a gigantic system of misrepresentation. It is misrepresenting the solvency of large banks and financial firms in debt to banks. The FED is doing its best to conceal the degree of risk and uncertainty in the capital markets. Central banks around the world are cooperating with the FED. This is an international effort by central bankers to deceive the public. To the extent that this deception is working, investor confidence will increase.*

On April 15, 2008, the FED held $866 billion in assets, which served as the monetary base for the nation. On April 15, 2009, it held $2.2 trillion! "

These increases are the same as giving more heroin to a sick addict. See more on inflation below.

Some say the Fed should be eliminated because it is a preposterous, damaging, and unconstitutional scheme. Others prefer to just reform it (audits, transparency, etc.). Steve Forbes' flawed book 'Money' (June, 2014) wants the Fed's FOMC to 'manage' the price of gold to keep it 'stable', and with no redeemability! This bashes the concepts of; 1. free market value, and 2. paper notes as just claim checks for gold, which **is** the money! (more on p. 54). I am in the 'Abolish the Fed' camp, and add that we should convert to gold money as discussed in Chapter 3. If we convert to the gold standard, the world will soon follow as fake money is refused by Sellers; a reverse form of; a) Gresham's Law (without legal tender laws), and b) Nixon's cut of the dollar's tie to gold in 1971. In this case, good money drives out bad. This would end the justification by all governments for money control and manipulation groups such as central banks worldwide, the BIS, World Bank, IMF, FDIC, legal tender laws, etc., all of which should be abolished.
Yellen and her pals worldwide would need to look for useful, productive, honest work. Good riddance!

The above heroin analogy sends the message that you will always get counter-productive conduct when you flood a system (nation, industry, family) with money.

The solution is to use real money (made of a commodity such as gold) and free markets so there is a stable supply and value of money, and 1. Thus not enough funding for wars and other corrupt deals, and 2. Failing deals aren't funded for long (with fiat money, government deals usually get MORE money when in trouble!). Not perfect, but many times better results (peace, prosperity, justice, etc.) than produced by government 'management' and meddling (intervention in the free market)!

'Monopoly' Money and Legal Tender Laws

Alan Greenspan was Chairman of the Federal Reserve System from 1987 to 2006 and was thus the chief, self-serving, 'pusher, dealer' of heroin money (excessive increase in money supply) into the US economy. He did this to keep his job (the Chm. is appointed by the President every 4 years) with full knowledge of, a) the risk of 'distortions' that the equally complicit Congress and Presidents would use it for (war costs, cheap loans for houses), and b) the resulting reduction in value (purchasing power vs. other currencies) of the USD. His meek excuse in Nov-2008 that: 'I erred in trusting the free market' is a lie, and he should be treated as a self-serving liar. He knew he was doing harm, as all heroin pushers do. I remember being asked sometime in about 1995 whether I thought Greenspan was doing a good job. I replied that 'It's not a matter of who has the job, I don't want the Fed to exist!' Congressional 'leaders' like Sen. Dodd and Rep. Frank deserve equal shame, plus others. Only a few people in Congress (Senators Hagel, McCain, Dole and others, and Rep. Paul) raised the red flag in the 2000 to 2005 period about the risks of excessive and fake money, but they were ignored. The crash of Oct-2008 was the result!

M-0,1,2,3; The Fed measures the quantity of U.S. money ('money supply') worldwide in four ways, in order of liquidity (how close it is to cash): M0= basic money supply (Fed Notes and coins = currency, cash), M1 = M0 + checking account deposits, M2 = M1 + near-money (savings accounts, mutual funds, etc; quick conversion to money), and M3 = M2 + large time-deposits (over $100k). They stopped publishing M3 in 2006 claiming high costs, but do they actually have something to hide? Private sources estimated M3 at $14 trillion in mid 2010, of which $6 trill. was overseas. Less than ten percent of M1 is coins or paper (= 'currency'). The rest is only in electronic form on computers.

In addition to creating the Fed, the government tampers with money in other ways, such as **'Legal Tender' laws.** Early controls, such as Art.1, Sec. 10 of the Constitution shown below, were used to assure that only 'real' commodity-based money was produced by the government, but politicians find ways to avoid these limits. Ignoring the Constitution is a convenient method, and no one seems to mind! Later, laws were designed to force people to accept fake money, such as Civil War 'Greenbacks', rather than insist on gold, etc. This forced Sellers to accept government money when offered (tendered) if they wanted legal recognition of deals (i.e., enforceable in court). These laws are usually a sign of weakness and fraud in a monetary system.
Another case of serious tampering occurred when FDR issued the Gold Recall Act (illegal Executive Order 6102) in 1933 that made it illegal for US citizens to own gold anywhere in the world, except for jewelry, and rare coins. This was codified by the Gold Reserve Act of 1934. It demonetized gold, and increased the government holdings. There are two explanations for this action:
1. The 'official' reason is that FDR was worried because foreign nations were redeeming their paper USD to gold

because they knew the U.S. was running out of it. That was true, but it was only part of the plan. To replenish the government supply the people were forced to sell it to the government in exchange for the going rate of $20.67 of paper Fed Notes per ounce. But after he had the gold, he increased the 'official' price to $35 oz ! (a bonus for the government !). The Act also voided contracts, and prohibited new ones, that called for settlement in gold (a 'gold clause').These restrictions on gold ownership were weakened for years, then ended by Pres. Ford in 1975.
2. A hidden reason is that FDR wanted to create new money to pay for his planned New Deal programs so used the above confiscation and restrictions as a tricky way to end the right of citizens to redeem paper notes for gold. Then he could create all the money he wanted!

The Act also established the **Exchange Stabilization Fund (ESF)**, which is still active. Initially funded by the above 'bonus' from gold confiscation, it had assets of $51.2 bill. as of June-2008. Its function is to use this special fund to: a. purchase or sell foreign currencies (manipulate the market!), b. hold U.S. foreign exchange and IMF-created 'Special Drawing Rights' (SDR); only used between nations) assets, and c. to provide financing to foreign governments, all aimed at bringing stability to the foreign exchange market (read, 'manipulate it to suit the US'). There is strong evidence that it was used in the 1990s to intervene (i.e., sell US gold) in the public gold market to suppress the price of gold (a high gold price makes fiat money look bad), and again in 2011 and 2012 (took gold from $1,900 oz. in Sep-2011 to $1,225 in Jan-2014). The Sec. of the Treasury has broad discretion in use of the money, and only his signature is required, and the transactions are not made known, even to Congress. We need to audit the Fed to reveal how much gold they still have, and of what quality. If it is much lower than the 8,134 tonnes the Fed claims to have, there will be a crash in value of the USD!!

In Jan-2013 Germany asked for return the 300 tonnes of gold it had stored in the Fed vault in New York (some say they did it because they were annoyed by the above secret price meddling in 2011). It is scheduled to be complete by 2020; 7 years! Why so long? In earlier attempts to verify the existence of its gold, the Fed only allowed Germans to take a peek into the vault, but no audit. Is it there, or has it been used for ESF dealing, leased, etc. Fortunately they cancelled their request.

While FDRs'1933 confiscation of gold effectively ended redeemability of paper 'money' for gold by mere people, the 1944 **'Bretton Woods** Agreement'** (an update of the 1922 "Genoa Plan') made it formal. This deal is named for the resort area in NH where major nations met to arrange world money 'management' in July, 1944. They set rules to: 1) Allow only nations to redeem paper for gold between each other (not people; thus a form of the Gold Bullion Exchange standard), 2) Create the International Monetary Fund (IMF; imf.org) to handle its foreign exchange transactions, 3) Create the World Bank (worldbank.org) to make loans to developing nations to reduce poverty (or bribe dictators), and 4) **Set the USD as the 'official' (not determined by market usage) worlds' reserve currency**, with a fixed value of $35 per troy ounce of gold.

The US engaged in so much monetary inflation (expansion of the money supply) after WW2 the USD lost much of its value, and due to high spending there, flooded Europe with so-called 'Euro-dollars'. France finally started demanding gold redemption for most of their paper dollars, which peaked in 1965 when Valerie Giscard d'Estaing (de Gaulle's Finance Minister) described the U.S. as having an 'exorbitant privilege' as the world's reserve currency, because it allowed us to pay our debts with money created out of thin air. Nixon soon refused to remit gold to any nation (we were running out), and then abrogated Bretton Woods on Aug. 15, 1971, setting the dollar 'afloat' with no redeemability. The Smithsonian Agreement was signed in Dec-1971, with gold set at $38 oz., in a vain attempt to continue the game. It failed in Feb-1973, and all nations went 'fiat' and made money out of thin air! The world money supply has soared ever since!

Figure 1: Purchasing Power (PP) of the US Dollar

The Incredible Shrinking Dollar — Down 95%

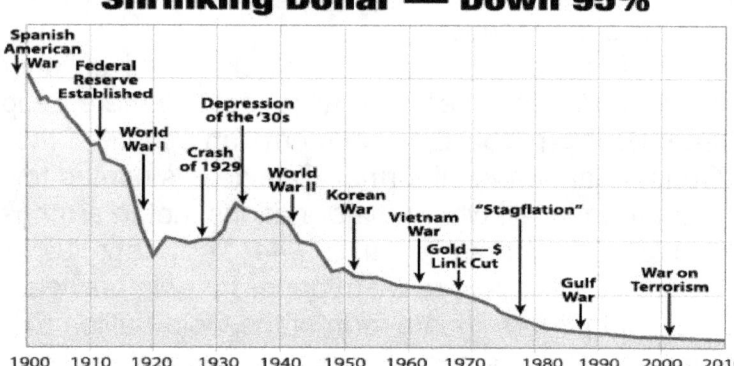

When dollars only buy 5% of what they used to, even having $1 million hardly counts as 'rich' anymore.

Source: Byron King, www.agorafinancial.com

Figures 1 and 2 offer a graphic look at the decline in PP of the USD, as the money supply is increased by the Fed.

Since 1971, the USD has had a floating exchange rate, which means that its value vis-à-vis other currencies is allowed to fluctuate and is determined, on a 'relative' basis, by the foreign exchange rate. In March, 1972, the US Dollar Index (USDX) was set up to measure the value of the United States dollar relative to a basket of foreign currencies (more on p. 100). It started at 100.000 and hit a low of 70.698 in March-2008. On an 'absolute' basis (purchasing power; PP), all world currencies have declined

44

in value since 1971, some faster than others depending on the strength of their economy and their amount of monetary inflation (increase in money supply). While the Fed on ly controls M0 (cash), I use M1 charts (M0 plus checking accounts) because it better reflects liquidity of the economy. (see p. 41 for definitions)

It is considered 'normal' for a country to increase its' money supply by 1 to 3% per year. Figure 2 shows how the M1 money supply increased rapidly with former Fed Chm. Bernanke's 'spike' in mid-2008 (reaching 15%), then due to 'Quantitative Easing' (create new money) hit 20% in mid-2011. The QE continued (with minor 'tapering') until it ended in Oct., 2014. Note that M1 has grown from about $1,400 bn in Jan-2008 to $2,800 bn in Nov-2014, a 100% increase in 6.9 years (14.5% per year!), with a peak of 21% in mid-2011! Much of it has been retained as bank reserves (they get interest from the Fed !!), so price inflation will come. The above Fed 'favors to businesses' end up as a hidden 'inflation tax' on US citizens.

Figure 2: U.S. Money Supply (M1); 1958 to 2018 (Billions)

(Source; https://tradingeconomics.com/united-states/money-supply-m1)

See p.41 for definitions of M-0, 1, 2, 3.
 M1 was $400 Billion. in Jan-1980, $700 Bn. in Jan-1990,
$1,000 B in Jan-2000, $ 2,000 in Jan-2010, and $3,614 in
Dec-2017.(Source; https://images.search.yahoo.com)

Analysis of Figure 2: The Federal Reserve System
started in 1913, helped fund WW1, did large M0 increase in
early 1920s to help England after WW1, then reduced M0
quickly due to market frenzy in mid '20s, a major cause of
the 1929 depression. The Fed increased M0 to fund WW2,
and increased it in the '80s as a stimulant after '80-81'
recession, which led to the 'dot.com bubble' in the '90s.
Interest rates were reduced by Greenspan in 2000 to 2006
to boost housing and recover from the dot.com bubble
crash in March-2000.
The Fed destroys the value of our money by excessive
expansion of the money supply ('monetary inflation') and
other meddling.

Figure 3: Gold prices in USD per ounce, 2008-2018
(Dollars shown are the current value for each year)

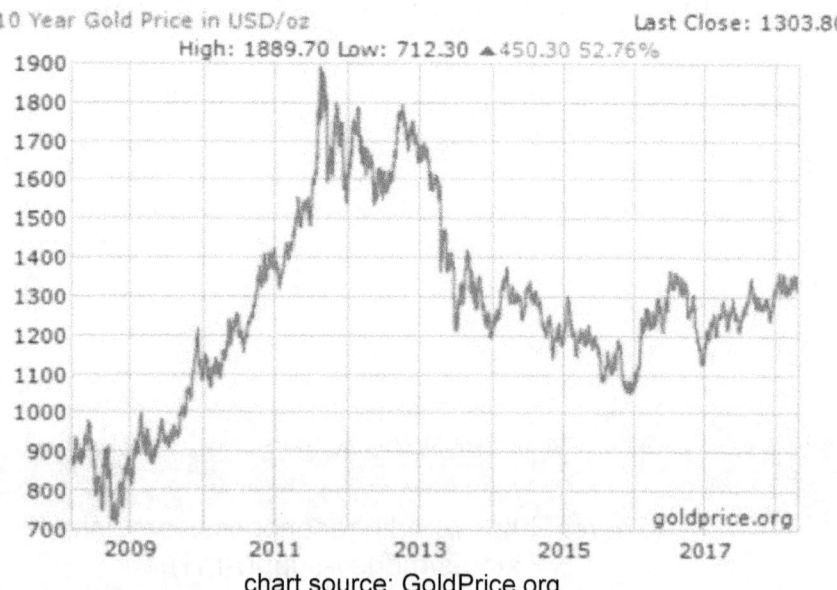

chart source: GoldPrice.org

Analysis of Figure 3: This figure shows historical gold prices in 2017 dollars, according to Bureau of Labor Statistics (Problem; their formula is adjusted to minimize inflation, thus reduce government payment increase based on inflation –such as Social Security-). It is helpful to see trends in constant dollars, to get the proper sense of change due to price inflation. The price spike in 1980 was $800 in 'nominal (the current) prices.

Summary: As shown in Figure 1, the US dollar has lost over 95% of its purchasing power since 1913, including loss of over 80% since 1971 (when Nixon cut ties to gold), due to excessive monetary inflation by the Fed (creating new money for the government to pay bills). This has been the main cause of the 2,000 % increase (20X) in prices since 1913, and 10X since 1971. We can all remember that a family car cost about $2,000 in the 70s, but is $20,000 today! Excessive money creation by banks prior to 1913 resulted in short-term inflation and 'panics' (runs on insolvent banks), but after 1913 the Fed facilitated long-term abuse by bailing-out such banks in its' corrupt role as **'lender of last resort'**. This in turn caused what economists call the **'moral hazard'** (taking high risks with the expectation of a bailout if needed) of the banks taking excessive risks by seeking high profits since the early 1990s. This is called 'casino banking' ! Remember; **"All central banks are created by and for politicians and bankers, so neither runs out of money."**

The International USD

Internationally, the USD emerged as the world's primary reserve currency (good as gold) after WW1 because of our economic strength. When Nixon cut ties to gold in 1971 (and soon all other nations did) it retained its' reserve currency status because all fiat paper money (not redeemable for a commodity) is actually viewed as 'backed' by the economic strength of the issuing nation. Until 2007, the US was without question the world's strongest economy, and thus the USD was strong because it was viewed as a share in 'USA Inc.'.

Since ending redeemability of paper money for gold in 1971, the US, 1) increased the rate of expansion of its M0 money supply even more than most other 'developed' countries, and 2) borrowed and spent to excess. Thus the dollars' value has decreased (and prices increased) rapidly ever since on both the;
 1) international exchange basis (about 4:1 against western Europe 'legacy' currencies from 1971 to 1999, then a loss of about 2:1 against the Euro from 1999 to 2008; 0.8 to 1.5 USD per Euro !), and
 2) by about 10:1 domestically (price increase of cars, pizza, etc.; things not subsidized or under price controls, or reduced due to new technology).
Thus our 'share of USA Inc.' money is decreasing in value and confidence as viewed by other nations, and they are seeking less dependency on the USD as the primary world reserve currency (see BRICS, p. 54). Loss, or a major reduction, of our reserve currency status will reduce or end our ability to; 1) create new money, and 2) borrow at low rates, to pay our bills at home and to other countries, and could result in a crash (loss of 50% or more of purchasing power in a few weeks) of the USD as international business flees to other currencies!!

All empires fail in part due to running out of purchasing power when their fake money becomes almost worthless. The failed empires of Rome, Italy, Spain, France, England, USSR, etc. are examples. Another sign of failing is decadence of the citizens. Look at how the content of TV, movies, and magazines have changed since the '50s, with more sex, violence and cursing.

Starting in the late '90s, Pres. Clinton and Rep. Barney Frank (the worst mortgage abusers) pushed Fannie and Freddie to 'help the poor' (and 'vote for me') by making more subprime loans, many of which were then sold to Wall Street to be securitized.

Foreign banks and investors happily bought trillions of dollars of these securities because they were primarily based on US real estate, had high interest income, and were apparently backed by the US government. The process was corrupt from the start, but was pushed by Congress and Wall Street elites. As the false prosperity slowed, and caused loss of US jobs, then mortgage foreclosures, these fake securities lost value, and the worldwide crash started in late 2008.

Euro Woes
From the beginning of the Greek debt crisis in April 2010, the Greek bailout has been about saving the banks that had purchased the Greek government's IOUs. The member states must be provided with euros, so that they can continue to make interest payments to the banks. Mario Draghi, an Italian banker and economist, succeeded Jean-Claude Trichet as the President of the European Central Bank (ECB) on 1 November 2011. He was expected to be aggressive in centralizing financial planning in the Eurozone. Despite a charter rule against it, in Jan-2015 he announced a major plan to have the European Central Bank (ECB) spend 1.1 tn euros on Eurozone government bonds which caused borrowing rates to drop (as planned; to attract investments), and drove the euro lower against the USD.

Another disaster struck on March 17, 2013 when the Eurozone announced a €10 bn 'bail-in' (a new term) of major Cyprus banks, that would be paid for by a 'tax' on deposits.

At the G20 (G20.org, the twenty largest nations), annual meeting in Turkey in Nov-2015 they discussed Syria, ISIS, and the migrant crisis in the wake of the recent terrorist attack in Paris, France, and currency issues.

The worldwide central bank efforts to make fiat currencies work are doomed, and should be, because they exist (despite PR and Lies to the contrary) only to serve banksters and politicians. The falling Euro drew special concern. Many U.S. banks are exposed to the Eurozone problems, and could be hurt; We'll see.

Avoiding the U.S. Dollar: The trend is to use less of the USD as a 'reserve currency' for international transactions. This will; 1. Reduce demand for dollars, and result in a major (50 to 80% ?) drop in value, and 2. Limit the USA's ability to get USD denominated loans at low rates (by selling bonds), and then repay them with newly created dollars.

Countries we buy imports from (China leads) accumulate billions of USD and buy our T-bills to get some interest (this also helps fund future purchases by the U.S.). This is a re-cycling of fake money, with interest paid by fake money, with all parties hoping it will last forever! Foreign nations that hold large amounts of USD-denominated assets (mostly bonds) are getting nervous that the USD will drop in value, so they are looking for ways to avoid dependency on, and ownership of, USDs. A flight to safety is starting, and could lead to a collapse in USD value.

China Sells U.S. Bonds and Buys Gold

See Figure 4 about selling bonds, and Table 2 about buying gold. This is a huge pattern of avoiding the USD! **The world is now selling the dollar at unprecedented rates,** which brings up a troubling question: **Where will that inflation now go?**
The answer? It's going to stay right here in the United States and eventually settle into our CPI. Most likely, they will take it out of us by inflating our dollars and we will pay for it through rising prices.

The gold listed for each of the countries in Table 2 may not be physically stored in the country shown. **An audit is needed** for all central banks, including 'counting twice' as part of leasing (by both owner & holder; or leaser & lessor)

Table 2: Top Ten Holders of Gold

As of August, 2018, in metric tonnes

USA	8,133.5	
Germany	3,369.9	
IMF	2,814.0	
Italy	2,451.8	
France	2,436.0	
Russia	1,944.0	(added 1,233 since 2012)
China	1,842.6	(added 789 since 2012)
Switzerland	1,040.0	
Japan	765.2	
Netherlands	612.5	
India	561.9	
Turkey	525.8	

(Source: World Gold Council, Gold.org, Statista.com, and https://en.wikipedia.org/wiki/Gold_reserve)

Many nations started heavy buying in 2008, when they felt the QE crash was over. Notice that Canada has no gold. They sold it due to lack of interest income, and hold bonds instead (mostly USA).

Fake money requires market demand to support its' purchasing power (PP). Gold is safe from complete loss, and this is why the Russian central bank has added 779 metric tons of the metal in the past decade, and China has added 1,656 metric tonnes since 2009! Based on these gold purchases, maybe China and Russia may be planning to destroy the petrodollar system by using gold as money, and thus crash the U.S. economy by ending the USD's role as the primary reserve currency?

The financial beauty of gold is that it tends to increase in purchasing power (PP, by weight of 24ct) over time, due to a near-fixed supply and increased demand (growing economies), while other forms of savings decline in PP as they inflated away. holdings in Figure 4.

Figure 4

The Tide Turns

Net foreign official purchases of U.S. Treasury notes and bonds, 12-month rolling sums

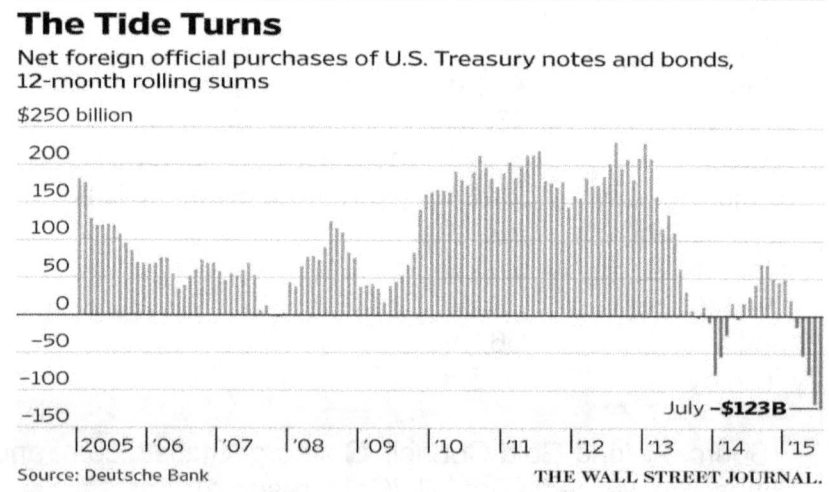

Source: Deutsche Bank

THE WALL STREET JOURNAL.

Figure 4 shows the world-wide sell-off of Treasuries, and thus our decreasing ability to export inflation. You can see how we were buffered by foreign governments and banks, China being the most significant, through the QE years. China held $1.32 tn of treasuries in Nov-2013 and reduced to $1.258 tn by Oct-2015.

China, Russia, BRICS, and the Petro-Yuan: China and Russia suggested at the Jan-2009 'World Economic Forum' in Davos that a new system is needed to replace the USD as the world's primary reserve currency, then they agreed to trade in their own currencies. In Aug-2011, China and France agreed to form a task force to discuss how the **Yuan could become part of the SDR** (see Glossary). It is said they want 20% USD (was 42%), 20% Yuan, 20% Yen, 20% Euro, and 20% Pound Sterling. In Dec-2011 China and Japan agreed to trade in their own currencies. In Jan-2012 Iran said it would sell oil to India in Rupees. China holds $1.3 trillions of USD denominated bonds and other assets, and doesn't want the USD to crash. Is this why in Feb-2013, China's central bankers suggest the world is moving "to a '1+4' system, with the greenback serving as the anchor of global payments, supplemented by 'four smaller reserve currencies' – the euro, sterling, yen and yuan." In any combination of the above trends, the USD is sliding down, and could lose over 50% of its' PP! Another reason some countries, especially Russia, want to create a new financial system is to end the US ability to impose political sanctions by restricting use of the US system.

BRICS: The first BRICS summit (Brazil, Russia, India, China, and South Africa) was held in Yekaterinburg, Russia, in 2009. They started trading with each other in their own currencies in 2011, thus reducing demand for the USD, and speeding its fall in value! At the July-2014 sixth summit of the BRICS in Brazil they started funding of **two multilateral financial institutions** designed to erode the dominance of the World Bank and International Monetary Fund (IMF) as arbiters of the global economic system. Namely: 1) A $100 billion **New Development Bank'** (like the World Bank), and 2) a Reserve Currency Fund (like the IMF) worth another $100 billion.

China Seeks Power: Huge changes in China's economic plans were made when Deng Xiaoping was Premier from 1978 to 1989. He led a remarkably successful economic reform program which greatly improved the material welfare (income and savings) of the majority of the Chinese people. Most changes were in more secure personal and property rights, which gave the people **incentive** to work hard and innovate. China has grown in activity and rewards in both their domestic and international trade. Todays' leaders follow his policies and China ROLLS !! Sadly, the Communist control of personal affairs is still there.

They made a major announcement on Oct. 24, 2014 with the creation the **Asian Infrastructure Investment Bank (AiiBank.org)**, a multilateral development bank to provide finance to infrastructure projects in the Asia region. AIIB is regarded by some as a rival for the IMF, the World Bank and the Asian Development Bank (ADB), which are dominated by developed countries like the United States. As of April 15, 2015, almost all Asian countries and most major countries outside Asia (total of 50) had joined the AIIB, except the US, Japan (which dominated the ADB) and Canada. North Korea's and Taiwan's applications for Prospective Founding Member (PFM) were rejected. The rush of our 'friends' in Europe to join is an indication of China's growing economic power. It is not clear which currency the AIIB will use. It could be the Yuan, or even the

IMF SDR, with the Yuan included. Either choice would reduce the USD dominance as a reserve currency, an ominous step toward collapse of the US economy!! iOn Nov. 13, 2015, IMF chief Christine Lagarde said the fund now deemed the yuan "meets the requirements to be a 'freely usable' currency" -- a key hurdle to joining the yen, dollar, pound, and euro as a leading unit in international trade. This implied the yuan (same as 'Renminbi', RMB) could be formally admitted to the IMF's "special drawing rights" currency basket at the IMFs' Nov. 30, 2015 meeting in Sweden. On Monday, Nov. 30, 2015, the IMF announced their approval of the Chinese renminbi as one of the world's main central bank reserve currencies, and part of the SDR. Minor changes in the percent of each currency in the SDR left the USA the same at 42, China now 11, and reductions for Yen 9.4 to 8, Euro 39 to 31, and the UK pound 11 to 8. The changes took effect in Oct-2016.

The IMF decision will help pave the way for broader use of the renminbi in trade and finance, securing China's standing as a global economic power. Chinese leaders view it as a giant step up for their place in world economics! The trouble is that much of the increase in demand for the yuan/renminbi will reduce demand for the USD, and its' purchasing power will fall even faster. Peter Schiff (SchiffGold.com) said; 'Another issue is a possible Chinese move to un-peg the yuan from the dollar, which could set off an earthquake.

When the Chinese decided to abandon their peg both for the Hong Kong dollar and the yuan – that is going to be a 10.0 on the Richter scale of economic activity. That is going to be huge. This time, it's going to be the dollar that takes it on the chin.'

To gain even more credibility, China has announced their current holdings of gold, which have been secret since revealed as 1,054 tonnes in 2009. As shown in Table 2, they have 1,843 tonnes now, which is #5 on the list of nations, with USA #1 at 8,134. (probably much less due to sales and hypothecation –using as collateral for loans-). Note Russia is just behind with 1,829 !

Despite the above good news, China has problems. David Stockman wrote on Dec. 1. 2015; *'At the time of the 2008 crisis, China's official GDP was about $5 trillion and its total public and private credit market debt was roughly $8 trillion. Since then, debt has soared to $30 trillion while GDP has doubled. And that's only when you count the massive outlays for white elephants and malinvestments (empty apartments and roads, etc.) which get counted as fixed asset spending.*

So at minimum, China has borrowed $4.50 for every new dollar of reported GDP, and far more than that when it comes to the production of sustainable wealth. Indeed, everything is so massively overbuilt in China - from unused airports to empty malls and luxury apartments to redundant coal mines, steel plants, cement kilns, auto plants, solar farms and much, much more - that more borrowing and construction is absolutely pointless.

It will only add to the downward pressure on prices, rents and profits, thereby insuring that trillions of bad debts will eventually implode. And that, in turn, will prolong the CapEx depression, which is the inexorable flip-side of the credit driven investment spree that has so massively bloated and deformed China's economy' (from; DavidStockmanscontracorner.com).'

The 2017 BRICS Summit was held in September in Xiamen in the eastern China province of Fujian. Chinas plans for creating a Petro-Yuan and making Yuan bonds (Yuan is same as Renminbi) available on more international markets (required to be in the IMF SDR basket of currencies were discussed.

With the increased strength of gold 'backing' (Table 2), on March 26, 2018 , **China announced that starting on April 6, 2018, it would issue gold-backed petro bonds denominated in the YUAN, and sure enough they did ! This 'Petro-Yuan' is a huge step toward displacing the USD from its' dominant petro-Dollar and arrogance**. Time will tell, but it's off to o good start with many purchases. The USD is used for most oil transactions (the Petro-Dollar); which keeps its' value up. To use other currency, (like Euro or gold) is a death sentence; note Saddam Hussein and M. Gadaffi.

Vladimir Putin, at the 11th meeting of the **Valdai International Discussion Club** in Sochi, also on Oct.24, 2014, said, *" Russia is making strides in assembling a massive new trading bloc known as the **Eurasian Union**. When it opened for business on January 1, 2015, Russia, Belarus, and Kazakhstan became a barrier-free market with 170 million people and a GDP of $2.7 trillion.."* The Union will further reduce demand for the USD, and thus reduce its' value (purchasing power).

USA Problems: The US economic problems have been brewing since extreme excess of the US dollar creation started in 1971 with Nixon's cutting of its last link to gold. With all this fake money to play with, Congress showed its willingness to offer loans and gifts to bailout companies, industries and nations who were in trouble (and could produce votes and campaign donations. This largesse created the 'moral hazard' of firms taking big risks on the assumption they would be bailed out if needed, and, along with lax regulation and false credit ratings, led to the crash that started in 2007. It also spawned lies from the government to cover-up the damage caused by their spending and money-meddling!

James Quinn, of The Burning Platform.com, wrote on Nov 7, 2015 ; "There were a few different stories coming out over the last few days that reveal the true nature of government and the apparatchiks who use disinformation, devious machinations, fraudulent accounting, and taxpayer money to cover up their criminality, lies, and the true state of the American economy. The use of government accounting tricks to obscure the truth about our dire financial straits is designed to keep the masses sedated and confused."

The rush of home loan defaults and bank problems started in late 2007, and peaked in Sep-2008. The underlying cause was Fed manipulation of interest rates, as described above. Using the Quantitative Easing (QE) program), an excessive supply of low-interest money was (and still is) delivered to banks by the Fed and its pals at FreddieMac and FannieMae. This is the 'mother's milk' of market distortion.

The World Economic Mess: It all comes back to how self-serving politicians, greedy 'casino' bankers, and government-loving liberals and academics, do more harm than good by 'managing' (meddling with) the natural free-market pricing, supply, and sound (metallic) money system. They get away with it because most people don't understand, or care about, the above economic and currency issues. They prefer bread and circuses, as many world economies crash!! SAD.

It has been a fun party since the Bretton Woods Agreement in 1944 made the USD the official 'worlds' reserve currency', and then our de facto (not official) reserve status since 1971, allowed us to create new money to pay our bills, and borrow to excess. **But things are changing!** Other nations are creating their own banking settlement networks (re less dependent on the USA!

Notes

Chapter 3: Use of Gold Coins, and Redeemable Paper Notes, as Money

History shows us that when countries use sound money (such as gold coins, or paper and base-metal tokens as redeemable receipts for gold) they have zero or low price inflation, zero or minor 'cycles' of economic panic or depression, and more peace, liberty, and prosperity (smaller governments, less war). For example, the number of grams of gold needed to buy a barrel of oil, or a man's suit, has been very steady over the years. Thus, we would expect all countries to use sound money, except the leaders want more money than they can get by just taxing, especially for wars. They want a way to create money 'out of thin air'. Fiat paper money (not redeemable for gold; we call ours 'Federal Reserve Notes') serves this purpose. Even when some level of redeemability exists, governments often 'suspend' it during wars (the US did for the Revolutionary, 1812, and Civil wars), and then must be pushed to restore it (often with less value). Using a valuable commodity as money solves these problems.

Why Gold?
All forms of money serve as a 'medium of exchange', 'unit of account', and 'store of value', which makes it convenient and flexible compared to barter. Think of commodity money as just a step up from barter, but with the flexibility of using it to buy anything.

Key Point: Note that when a valuable commodity (such as gold) is used as money -'monetization of gold'-, the money has market value equal to the goods or services in the transaction. **Commodity money is not just a symbol (face value). The material it is made of has market value (based on demand for industrial and consumer**

uses). Thus it can also be a 'store of value' (savings; keep some for later use), even when not used as money (often called 'intrinsic value').

Critics of the gold standard point out that gold's price varies widely. In his Dec. 3, 2011 report, Gary North (garynorth.com) says: *'Excuse me? The gold market today establishes the price of gold in terms of fiat money systems run by central banks. So, the price of gold as denominated in fiat money varies mainly because the value of currencies fluctuates wildly.'*

Two more benefits of using commodity money are to;
1. Limit excessive expansion of the money supply (inflation; loss of value) by the government (you can't create a commodity at little or no cost, like paper 'money'), and
2. Provide a market-based, and stable, store and measure of value.
This gold standard needs no government controls or 'management', except inspections (which could be by a private org) to verify mints indeed have the gold reserves they claim to for redemptions. The commodity could be (and has been) wheat, iron, diamonds, or pearls, but the market (users of money) usually chooses gold because it works best for the ten reasons shown on page 64. Thus, it will be used as the 'presumed market choice' in this book. Silver and copper supplies and costs are more volatile than gold (more new production, are consumed for industrial use, etc.), so are less attractive, but useable.

Paper 'money certificates' or 'notes' are not money but just 'claim checks' for gold money. Token coins (base metal) can be used as a convenience (cheap to make, light weight, avoid loss of gold due to wear, etc.), but users of this 'representative money' in a private –not government-monetary system, will insist it must be marked on its face as to how much gold it represents (weight and fineness) and be redeemable for that amount on demand by any bearer at the issuing bank or mint. Further, users will insist the bank or mint must disclose to the public (via lobby poster, mail to depositors, Internet web site, etc.) the weight and purity of gold it has on hand as 100% reserve (physically; no encumbering liens or leases) for redemption of paper notes and base-metal tokens, and the amount of this 'representative money' currently issued. Without these conditions, and in the absence of legal tender laws, people (the 'market') will not use such representative money, and will seek better money from another mint. Time deposits (savings) can be less than 100%, but such reserves must be declared to depositors, so they can bank elsewhere if they don't like the policy. **Competition will produce good money!**

When gold is used as money, it has no 'price' in dollars, yen, etc. Weight is the **unit of account** (such as milligrams). Sellers will set prices in weight of 24 ct gold (embossed on the coin).

There will be prices IN 'weight of 24 ct gold', but not OF gold! (Example; What is the price of a dollar?). Gold money will have an 'exchange rate' with other money, but not a 'price'. This will take some getting used to as we evolve to pricing in weight of gold.

Prof. Joseph Salerno (pace.edu) wrote two excellent articles on this topic: **1) 'A Substandard Golden Rule'**, in the 'Mises Daily' on May 29, 2013 (http://mises.org/daily/6442/A-Substandard-Golden-Rule), and **2) 'The Myth of the Unchanging Value of Gold'**, on Aug. 29, 2014 (http://mises.org/daily/6858/The-Myth-of-the-Unchanging-Value-of-Gold). He pans the faulty book 'Money' by Forbes-Ames which uses the Fed to 'manage' the price of gold, and ignores its' 'store of value'. Steve Forbes likes 'big government' so favors easy expansion of the money supply. Don Miller MD wrote a good article

Money can be in many forms, but this analysis will discuss metal coins and paper notes (currency).

A. Metal Coins, which can be of two types;

A1. 'Commodity', where they are partly or wholly made of a commodity such as gold or silver. Various coin values would have different amounts. For example, a small, round, gold disc could be forged into a hole in the center of a coin. This would allow testing to assure its purity and weight. The balance of the coin would be hard base metal or alloy, with the weight of precious metal the coin contains marked on it

Table 3: Why Gold is the Best Commodity for Coins

To achieve broad use, commodity coins must be made of, or contain, a material that has these

Ten Characteristics:

1) Rare, with a low amount in existence now, and limited new supply,
2) Malleable; can be pressed/stamped into coins,
3) Durable; Stable physically and chemically; doesn't break, rust, or rot; can be stored; lasts through much handling,
4) Easy to identify, and determine purity and weight,
5) Difficult or impossible to counterfeit,
6) Homogeneous; a piece is the same throughout,
7) Divisible into pieces; diamonds and pearls aren't,
8) High value per ounce; easy to handle, store, & transport
9) Acceptable to most Sellers; familiar and saleable,
10) Has market value when not used as money. Thus;
   a. is equal in value to the items in a transaction, and

b. is a store and measure of value.

The 'market' (users of money) has decided that gold fits these requirements best, but silver and copper can have a role in parallel, with no fixed ratios set as to value per gram (i.e., no bi-metallic standard). The coins must be valued and marked by weight of their precious metal content (such as 'milligrams'), or the amount they can be redeemed for. It is interesting to note that gold is not 'consumed' by economically unrecoverable uses (electronics, photography) as other commodities, including silver and copper, are. Thus except for wear, over 90% of all gold mined in history still exists (even if buried in a tomb).

Approximately 160,000 metric tonnes of gold have been mined in all history. Gold mined per year has increased from 2,332 tonnes in 2009 to 2,980 in 2013, so the above-ground supply is expanding at about 1.9% per annum, which is not enough to cause noticeable near-term inflation (less value per gram) of the money supply. The aggregate un-mined known 'useable, reachable' reserves of all the world's gold mining companies is approximately 45,000 tonnes, and ore quality (grams of gold per tonne of rock) is less for new mines, so new tonnes-per-year may decline.

There is always 'enough' gold for money, because if a nation's economy (GDP) grows faster than its gold supply, the increased demand will cause their gold for domestic transactions to **APPRECIATE** in purchasing power per ounce, which in turn cause deflation (lower prices). The same logic applies to the world economy. It is self-adjusting and needs no government meddling!

A2. 'Representative' (or 'Token'), where the tokens are made of base metals such as copper, aluminum, zinc, nickel, steel, and alloys, and are marked as redeemable to a certain weight and purity of a commodity such as gold or silver. These are useful for lower value transactions.

B. Paper Notes: A **'representative' note** is just a convenient (easy to carry, many values) 'receipt' or 'claim check' for precious metal, and must be; 1) Valued and marked by the weight or amount of the commodity it represents. No 'name', such as 'dollar', is needed, and 2) Redeemable for such commodity by the Bearer upon a demand to the Issuer (mint or bank) of the paper at Issuer's various premises, with such locations publicized (via Internet web site, sales literature, etc.).

The above Appreciation is a positive incentive to save, and avoid debt, a concept that people today have never seen because all nations use depreciating fiat money.

Appreciation of money's value under a gold standard is; a) ignored by most economists (they prefer 'flexible' fiat money; they do the flexing) and b) suppressed by, or unknown to, all politicians because they love paying debts and minimizing taxation by expanding the money supply with fake money - monetary inflation - and paying debts with low value, 'new' 'money'.

Gold money solves the problem of excessive imports causing loss of jobs due to off-shoring of factories. With the finite supply of real money (with strict reserves of gold for redemption), US importers will find themselves, and their banks, getting short of money, and import less. Demand will increase for domestic producers, a

nd the money will stay in the same country (see more at item 6 on p. 59). Free trade is good, unless importing is taken to extremes by the use of fake money. Note again, this can only happen if the fake money is also the world's reserve currency (until demoted!). Poor citizens in third-world countries which have little 'real money' to buy imports, will have incentive to work hard, innovate, and earn gold from exports.

To avoid future crashes we should cut taxes, end wars and empire, end all subsidies, end the unconstitutional and damaging (allows Federal meddling) Departments of Education, Homeland Security, Commerce, Agriculture, and others, and take broad measures to reduce government spending. After a recession, free-market capitalism (if we use it) can rise from the ashes, and produce honest, sustainable, jobs, peace, and prosperity. Sadly, many politicians prefer socialism, and that will just prolong the pain!

As of April 29, 2018 the Fed is writing about the virtues of 'electronic' money, with no cash. This would let them play their games, and avoids facing the crash of the USD value, or a mass acceptance of cryptocurrency..

I don't underestimate the difficulty of, and opposition to, a transition to gold as money. Some will say we should set less ambitious goals, but I say these lesser goals are just steps along the way and we must never stop striving for the ultimate goal of eradicating the government from our monetary system.

Maybe if we hit bottom hard enough (2019, 2025?) in the current recession, people and the government will start to listen to us 'real money' folks, and go for the gold.

Because the Fed gives it an unlimited supply of funding, the U.S. Federal government has become an arrogant master that dominates and abuses its citizens, the U.S. States, and other countries (by jerking the purse strings), while providing big incomes and privileges to those people and firms that have ready access to it. Our national disease is that it is deemed 'normal' to have the government supply whatever is 'nice', 'good', 'needed', or 'wanted', and most people want/expect 'somebody else' to pay for it ('the rich'). This parasitic mode of living is immoral and unsustainable, and reveals the classic signs of decadence in a failing empire.

Fighting the system is hard, but I predict Ghandhis' aphorism will prevail: **"First they ignore you, then they ridicule you, then they fight you, then you win."**

As the world moves to gold-as-money, names like 'Dollars' can be eliminated and 'weight' (grams, etc.) will rule as the unit of account for pricing! Since the U.S. has trillions of fiat 'dollars' in circulation worldwide, the market value of a USD for conversion (trade-in) purposes will be a small fraction of an ounce. This implies that a minimum dollar amount may be required for an owner to redeem representative money for physical gold, since the tiny physical size of gold per dollar would be a problem in handling and measuring. If it were not a secret as to how much gold the government has at Fort Knox, the IMF, and in Federal Reserve facilities, a better estimate could be made. For a plan to convert the USD to gold, see the 'Five Step Plan' in Chapter 4 of my book 'Monetary Revolution USA'. Get it at Amazon,com.

Benefits of a Gold-Money World

In summary, we can expect the following benefits when the new gold money becomes legal:

1. More Peace: Wars are very expensive. The absence of an unlimited supply of fake money will inhibit the starting of wars; Diplomacy will be used instead. Imperialistic aggressors will have trouble getting funded.

2. More Prosperity: Gold money will increase in value (purchasing power) if percent economic growth exceeds the percent addition of newly mined gold. Savings will be rewarded, more money value will be available for investments, and managers and entrepreneurs can plan better.

3. Less Government: Governments need money to grow. Taxation has its limits, and in the absence of the unlimited supply of fake money, government programs, staffing, and spending will be limited. There will be less intervention in, and control of, our lives and work. More Liberty, Peace, and Prosperity will be the dividends.

4. Stable Money Value (Purchasing Power): When gold has a price in dollars, etc., the price goes up as the value of the fiat dollar falls. Governments hate this exposure! Our government intervened in 2011 to sell gold (see ESF p. 42) and change interest rates, etc. to force the gold price down (from $1,900 oz. in Sep-2011 to $1,090 on Nov. 8, 2015) on the 'paper' market of ETFs, etc. The Fed also worked with their 'bankster buddies' (they saved them because they need them!) to manipulate the gold market with massive volumes of illegal 'naked shorts', as described in Dr. P.C. Roberts and David Kranzler's Jan. 17, 2014 article http://www.paulcraigroberts.org/2014/01/17/hows-whys-gold-price-manipulation/. In their Jan. 30, 2014 article (http://www.paulcraigroberts.org/2014/01/30/fed-tapering/) he explained how the Fed is now facing a decision on whether to support their 'buddy banks' with more QE, or the U.S. Dollar by 'tapering' QE, because both are failing. QE ended in Oct-2014. The Fed is 'between a rock and a hard place' of its own making. Despite this Fed meddling, the demand for owning physical ownership remains strong (especially in India and China). The price of gold will soar (due to demand) when the government runs out of gimmicks to suppress it. History and logic show us that when 'weight of gold' is the 'unit of account' for pricing, and there is no Fed to do politicized meddling, purchasing power and prices are stable.

5. Fewer and Smaller Business Cycles and Depressions: The 'highs' of major business cycles are caused by bad investments due to excessive availability of money (credit and currency); too many new dollars chasing a limited number of deals, many of which are high risk. The incentive is to 'do something' with the excessive money. With a limited supply of real gold money, any spending frenzies would soon run out of money to feed them, and the cycles would be small or none.

6. Fewer Jobs 'Off-Shored': Due major increase in US wage and benefit costs after WW2, starting in the '80s, factories were built in other nations where costs are lower (first Mexico, then China, India, etc.) and the jobs moved out of the US! The same applies to software, engineers, and production technology since the '90s. In addition, there is no limit to how much a country can import when it issues the world's primary reserve currency and can make it out of thin air. That's why our imports have soared since 1971 (when Nixon ended the dollar's tie to gold), and many of our factories have shut down. With gold as money, the importers run out of money, and local producers get the business. This is one of the self-regulating aspects of gold.

7. Fewer Sovereign Defaults and No Currency Devaluations: In the past, many nations have defaulted (stopped payments) on some or all of their debt when they could not pay the interest, and then devalued (reduced exchange value by major increase in money supply) their currency to increase exports. This robs lenders, and holders of the currency, and increases cost of imports. Argentina in 2002, and even the normally prudent Swiss in 2013, are examples. As with most government meddling, debasing the currency does more harm than good! When gold is used as money by all the major nations (and thus all nations must follow), there are no 'floating values' (exchange rates) between them (just weight of 24 ct gold) so the devalue option ends. This will give politicians incentive to keep their laws and economy more competitive (less spending, taxing, and regulations) to avoid more gold outflows (and less inflow) caused by reduced production and investment.

8. Less 'casino' banking: Banksters tend to ignore caution and engage in high risk-reward 'investments when; 1) money is 'plentiful, and 2) they can enjoy the 'moral hazard' of expecting a bailout (from the Fed) if their schemes fail. We can enjoy the above benefits, and avoid a crash of our economy if we **convert to gold-as-money!**

A Plan to Convert the USA to Gold as Money

Chapter 4 of **Daves' book 'Monetary Revolution USA'** has a detailed 'Five-Step Plan' to convert the USA to gold as money. This plan is a **'top down'** approach where Congress is required to change many laws (legal tender, Fed monopoly, etc.). This is very hard to implement, but a few Congressmen have tried. The new plan at the end of the same Chapter 4 is a **'bottom up'** approach where the States are the instigating party by authorizing gold and/or silver for use as near-money, and **not taxed as a commodity.** Of course, this is authorized by Article 1, Section 10 which requires that only gold and silver coin be used in payment of debts, but the Article also prohibits the States from coining money, and thus it remains only with the federal government. A way to use 'near money' having many characteristics of money) is needed in order to avoid a conflict with the Constitution.

The States of AZ, LA, NC, NV, OK, TX, and UT have announced plans to treat gold more like money by not taxing its' value changes as a commodity. A good first step! These plans, and for other States as they occur, are described in detail in the Aug-2017, and later editions, of my book '**Monetary Revolution USA**' (available at Amazon.com). See my essay on P. 95 below for a detailed plan to convert the USA to 'Gold as Money'.

To see my essays on various topics, go to ActivistPost.com, select 'Contributors' at top of the Home page, then scroll down to my name. Some of my articles are also shown on P. 89 to 97 below.

Chapter 4:   Investment Strategy:

WARNING: To avoid losses due to an expected major drop in the value (Purchasing Power) of the US Dollar; 1) sell most of your stocks, bonds, annuities, etc. (they can go to zero value when the USD fails), 2) buy Hard Assets such as precious metals, farm land, and residential real estate, 3) buy strong Foreign Assets and Currency, 4) work with a Wealth Management Planner (p. 82), and 5) consider a Trust Fund in a foreign jurisdiction. Time is running out before government controls are imposed to prevent the above changes!!

Chapters 1 to 3 explained how the USA money, banking, and securities systems started and works today, and how the abuse of these systems by politicians, 'banksters', and other 'interest groups' has caused the decline in strength of our money and economy. As stated in the Introduction, over 95% of Americans living today have never experienced a depression, or severe recession. Except for the 'bubble burst' losses in 2008, which has been temporarily repaired by massive increases in our money supply ('monetary inflation') called 'Quantitative Easing' by the Fed, all stock, bonds, and real estate investments have increased in price since their teen years, and most people expect it to continue. Americans tend to look at losses as minor 'corrections' or 'bumps' in the upward path. Well folks, the bad times are here, and investors need to 'wake up' and become aware that after decades of high spending and borrowing, the USA economy is now approaching the cliff of a crash in US Dollar value (over 50% loss), major investment losses, and consumer price increases (hyperinflation). In this chapter, I give you ideas on how to protect and grow your wealth during these perilous times.

As I write in May--2018, the US Dollar (USD) has lost 98% of its 1913 purchasing power (PP), and over 80% of its 1971 PP (the decline rate got worse after Nixon severed the USD tie to gold in 1971). Most investors judge values of stock by the prices listed by the various stock exchanges, and trends shown by the Dow Jones Industrial Average (an index of 30 US stocks published since 1896), and the 'S&P 500', but this ignores any change in the value (PP) of the currency in which the stock (or any other investment) is denominated. This brings a new meaning to 'diversification' of your investment portfolio. The new factors are; 1) Trends of change in currency value in the U.S. and other nations (and their politics), and conversion to a better currency when needed, 2) Inclusion of precious metals (PM) as an inflation hedge, and 3) Selection of a Wealth Manager to create your plan (Trust Fund, etc.) for more wealth, and less risk, taxation, and confiscation. More at #6 on p. 80.

Evaluating Five Key Ways to Invest

The five topics below focus on how to find and use info sources and strategies you may not have considered before.

1. Instead of just 'Price' (from 'Dow Jones' etc.), the 'Value', or 'Purchasing Power' (PP), of your investments is what you should want to increase. You can test changes in PP by tracking how much of a 'standard product' (ie, a common product with minimal exposure to politics, subsidies, tariffs, offshoring, price controls, and new technology), such as a cement block, a loaf of normal bread, a room at Motel 6, a Big Mac burger, etc. that your investment will buy. Price increases in these items are caused primarily by loss of currency PP. Don't use milk, eggs, or gasoline. They are distorted higher because of corn subsidies (and high demand due to the government pushing corn-based ethanol for gas), and wars in the middle-east. Radios and portable devices (pocket calculators, cell phones, iPads, etc.) are lower because of cheap integrated circuits, mass production, and offshoring of manufacturing. For a recent change, look back at the early 1970s, before the 1971 'no gold' floating USD inflation took effect. Notice that family cars cost about $2,000 and are about $20,000 today!; same for Motel 6 going from $6 to $50. To look back further, go to Figure 1 on P. 44 to see the 98% loss of USD PP since the Fed started in 1913.

The 'price' of your asset in currency 'X' may go up, but if the PP of the currency in which it is 'priced' falls by a greater percent, you have lost value. Again, foreign exchange markets are a good measure of 'relative' changes (one currency to another) in PP of currency, **but they may all be falling!** The 'absolute' PP is measured by how much of 'standard products' (not affected much by subsidies or politics) a currency unit will buy.

2. Domestic IRAs and 401(K)s have tax advantages, but; a) their contents can be confiscated by the government (US or other) and replaced with a high-risk, or near worthless, bond (Obama's 'MyRA' is a first step), or b) drop in value if the USD keeps falling, etc. This even applies to Gold IRAs because the IRS requires they must all be kept in their 'approved' vault in the 'Delaware Depository' in Wilmington which makes it easy for them to confiscate the gold.

3. The yield on CDs and bonds is negative if the PP of the currency in which they are denominated falls at a higher rate than the CD interest rate. (see #1 above)

4. The Dow Jones Industrial Averages (DJIA) may rise, but you need to consider how much of this is price inflation caused by falling currency value. This 'false happiness' caused the stock boom of the 1990s, and continues today because of the QE program. When the Fed increases the money supply (monetary inflation), each existing USD

75

becomes worth less (2 words!) and this means more USD are needed to buy any good or service (price inflation). For protection from losses due to failure of your broker, visit www.bulletproofshares.com.

5. Most important, all fiat money (not redeemable for a valuable commodity, and forced to use at face value by legal tender laws) eventually falls to little or nothing in value (purchasing power). As shown in Figure 1 on P. 44, the USD has lost 98% of its PP since the Fed started in 1913.

Key Point: Most investors don't consider all of the above five issues, so they become victims of falling currency values, and often don't even know it. You will read below the advantages of currency and nation diversification, and personal possession of bullion. Under duress, laws mean nothing to the government. Remember the Cyprus 'bail-ins' of 2013 (deposits were replaced by worthless bank shares).

Four Ideas for Strategy: Please consider the four ideas below as a supplement to all you know from strategy that most 'traditional' securities brokers promote;

1. Select a Wealth Manager who thinks beyond the 'conventional wisdom', and considers currency value risks, and government taxes and confiscation, to create your plan for more wealth. (see p. 82)
2. Watch trends in the purchasing power, based on the foreign exchange markets, of the currency in which your 'paper' assets are denominated,
3. Consider the possibility of taking 'physical possession' of commodities you own (such as gold; handy for storage because it is small in size for a high value), and
4. Know the politics (corruption, restrictions, etc.) of the nations whose securities, private business stocks, and currency you buy, or use for storage of PM.

For example, a key event occurred on July 1, 2014 when the U.S. activated the **Foreign Account Tax Compliance Act (FATCA; see Appendix, p. 89)** which will require all banks worldwide to file an egregious amount of forms and documents with the US government if they accept US citizens as clients. The foreign bank will be subject to a 30% withholding tax on any "withholdable payment" made to its proprietary account for failing to comply with FATCA. **Many banks are refusing to deal with US citizens, thus time is running out to freely 'internationalize' assets!**

Table 4 below shows the ranking of the Top 10 nations with 'strong' currencies and economies (stable and less likely to decline in value than others). Note that Japan and the Eurozone Bank are engaging in major monetary inflation and may fall off the list.

Table 4: Ranking of Nations with Strong Currencies

Country	Currency Code	Perform. vs Gold (10 yrs) %	Debt to GDP %	Balance of Trade (% of GDP)
1.Switzerland	CHF	29	46.7	9.4
2.Australia	AUD	27	27.1	-2.9
3.Canada	CAD	25	87.5	-2.6
4.Norway	NOK	25	49.6	14.6
5.Japan	JPY	24	236.0	3.1
6.China	RMB	21	27.2	5.2
7.Europe	EUR	20	80.O	-1.6
8.USA	USD	16	107.0	-3.7
9.UK	GBP	16	88.7	-1.8
10.India	INR	15	67.6	-1.7

(Source: SeekingAlpha.com/article/313342, Dec-2011 except Debt/GDP is Dec-2012; the same order in Jan-2015)
The trend is up (worse) for the Debt/GDP ratios of all countries except China, Australia, Switzerland, and Sweden (Sweden was 37.2% in Dec-2012, and is considered a strong currency). The Chilean economy has grown well since their conversion from a military dictatorship (Pinochet) in 1990, to democracy and free market policies. Their peso (CLP) has strengthened against the USD since 2004, and their Debt/GDP ratio is only 12%. Their stocks, currency and land are becoming attractive for purchase. Countries with the best combination of numbers in Table 3 will be attractive to investors seeking currency diversification. Note that negative trade balances and high debt-to-GDP are a warning of future decline.

As I write in Jan-2018, a US citizen can still buy Precious Metals (PM) without the government knowing (good, it's none of their business!), but as the USD falls, the government gets desperate for ways to protect itself from; 1) falling faster, or 2) citizen use of other currencies and PM, at home and abroad (see BRICS, P. 54).

Seven Ways to Acquire Precious Metals and Non-USD Currencies
For your convenience, some firms you can use are shown below. Some are 'contrarian', and not likely to be mentioned by mainstream, 'conventional', securities brokers. Search the Internet for others. Many offer newsletters.

1. Precious Metal Dealers; Shop-around; check on their 'premiums' (price above 'spot'), minimum order size, 'ship and insure' fees, etc.; SchiffGold.com (articles and radio info by Peter Schiff, and EuroPacificFunds.com), JMBullion.com, MoneyMetals.com, InvestmentRarities.com (newsletter), Caminocompany.com, Monex.com, JimsCoins.net, LearCapital.com, Apmex.com, Blanchardonline.com, HardAssetsAlliance.com (click on choices at top of HardAssets home page), GoldSilver.com (articles by Mike Maloney), MilesFranklin.com (articles by Andy. Hoffman), Gainesvillecoins.com, Goldmoney.com, SwissAmerica.com, GlobalGold.ch, Sgpmx.com, MerkGold.com, BGASC.com, and NWTmint.com. There are many others.

Here are some ideas for basic items to buy: When the USD crashes, pre-1965 US silver coins (see P. 18-20, 'junk silver'), and new government-issued bullion coins (such as gold or silver Eagles), will be useable as money (by weight and fineness/purity) because Sellers will know and trust their content (not true for bars). For example, if silver rises to $80 per oz (5 x May-2015 price) a pre-1965 dime (0.072 oz silver) will be worth $5.76, and a Silver Eagle (1 oz Silver) $80. Since 1986 the US Mint (www.usmint.gov) has issued a variety of gold, silver, and platinum bullion coins. As shown in Table 5 below, their face values are far below their bullion market value, and thus, though they are legal tender, are not used in commerce. Many US dealers sell the bullion, medallions, numismatic coins, and bars issued by various countries and private mints. Be careful, bars and ingots are easy to fake by plating base metal with a precious metal.

Table 5 shows some of the more popular bullion coins (all made by government mints). There are many more.

Table 5:   Popular Bullion Coins

Country ;	Name ;	Metal;	Sizes (troy oz.);	Face Values ($)
USA ;	Gold Eagle;	0.9167 Gold ;	1,1/2, 1/4, 1/10;	$50, 25, 10, 5
USA ;	Silver Eagle;	0.9999 Silver;	1 ;	$1
Canada;	Mapleleaf;	0.9999 Gold;	1,1/2, 1/4, 1/10;	C$20,10,5,1
So. Africa;	Krugerrand ;	0.9167 Gold;	1, 1/2, 1/4, 1/10;	no FV
P. R. China ;	Panda	0.9999 Gold ;	1, 1/2, 1/4, 1/10 ;	no FV

(Info- 24 carat = 0.9999 pure gold   22 carat = 0.9167 pure)

2. Precious Metal Storage: Once you own some precious metal (PM), where do you keep it? Most dealers work with domestic or foreign 'vault' firms you can use. 'Brinks' is highly rated. Some have their own (sgpmx.com). But most banks and commercial vaults are not safe (even overseas) because the U.S. government can use 'lockouts', bank 'holidays', 'Bail-ins' like Cyprus, or 'forced exchange' (like FDR in 1933) for bonds or fiat cash, etc. to prevent access by you. This is **'confiscation'** (theft?) they claim is legal based on the 1917 'Trading with the Enemy Act'!). If you keep it in your possession, it must also be safe from burglars. Most gun stores sell lockable cabinets. A somewhat bizarre, but useful, choice is to bury your PM in a sealed container in a private place such as your backyard. A two to four foot long piece of 4 or 6 inch diameter PVC pipe from your local hardware, with end-caps glued on, will work. Plant a bush over it and tell 2 trusted people where it is in case you die, or forget.

3. Precious Metal Mines: These are high risk/reward investments. Credible sources for info are:
a. Doug Casey CEO of Caseyresearch.com, and his staff, are world experts on PM mining; see Caseyresearch.com .

b. The EuroPac.net 'Gold Fund' (*EPGFX)* invests in precious metals, PM producers, PM exploration, and prospecting companies. See; EuroPacificFunds.com
c. 'Streetwise Reports' publishes 'The Gold Report', that includes info on mines at; theaureport.com/pub/htdocs/38.
d. Mining.com offers 'Global Mining News' and issues free reports on mining minerals and precious metals.
e. The 'World Mining Congress' (http://www.wmc.org.pl/) has members worldwide and holds annual conventions.
f. The 'World Gold Council' (www.gold.org) is a non-profit association of the world's leading gold mining companies, that promotes the use of gold.

4. Foreign Currencies and Equities:

 a. Euro Pacific Capital, Inc., (EuroPacificFunds.com, EuroPac.net) is a broker-dealer that offers a variety of services and products, including fifteen mutual funds they created (for 'nation diversity'), and precious metals. Look at all parts of the above sites for details. They promote geographic and currency diversification. (Note: Europacificbank.com cannot be used by US citizens)
 b. Have your assets protected by a foreign trust, before further currency controls are put in place to prevent it. A trust can be written so you give up ownership (thus minimize taxes) yet retain control, and is Multi-Generational. One type is a 'Charitable Remainder Trust'. The goal is to internationalize your assets in a tax efficient manner without losing control.
c. Merkinvestments.com offers 4 foreign currency funds (merkfunds.com), and reports. Also see vanguard.com
d. EverBank Financial Corp. (EVER, Everbank.com) is a U.S. bank that offers savings accounts denominated in foreign currencies. The EverBank **'Evolving Economies'** Certificate of Deposit (CD) diversifies your money into a basket of currencies that get stronger as the USD declines.
e. For exchange rate info, transfers, and brokerage, see Forex.com and usforex.com .

5. Crypto Currencies

Computer-based currency has evolved in an effort by users to avoid the restrictions and depreciation of fiat money from governments and banks. 'Bitcoin' was first, and now several more are available. Jeff Berwick at DollarVigilante.com has been very active in this market (Newsletter@DollarVigilante.com). See his video seminars at;
 https://dollarvigilante.com/nationless-private-bank?cfid=139 . The seminar shows the status of ten crypto currencies. For info about a large exchange see Coinbase.com.

Cryptos have made spectacular gains in value since Bitcoin started in 1990. However, my view is that since the current demand for crypto currencies is based primarily on problems with existing government fiat currencies, the demand for, and price of, cryptos will fall if; a) new commodity–based, gov't electronic, or 'basket' currencies appear, and b) abuse and fraud become part of crypto management (the Block Chain algorithm; a ledger) as it has with all non- commodity currency in the past. **All cryptos are created and managed by humans, and therein lies the risk of abuse.** Blockchains are also created by humans, and can be changed by them! For more info, visit;
http://www.investopedia.com/terms/b/blockchain.asp.

6. Wealth Management Consultants and Advisors

There are a variety of 'traditional', 'mainstream', financial planning firms, often part of banks or securities brokers. Their type of 'diversity' of your portfolio includes annuities, CDs, bonds, and stocks, but they are usually all denominated in US Dollars (USD), and thus subject to major loss of value (purchasing power); 1) due to interest rates being lower than price inflation, and 2) when (not if) the USD crashes. Because of the U.S. and world economic chaos, this book adds the diversity of 'internationalization', which includes geographic and currency diversification, and foreign legal structures (jurisdictions) to minimize taxation and controls. Read part 6 below, and Appendix part A.

The firms shown below have good reputations, and offer services consistent with the above paragraph. Check the Internet for more.

a. EuroPac.net, and EuroPacificFunds.com/about (Asset Management), CEO Peter Schiff. They have 15 funds that are either foreign-based (thus stock is not in USD), or US firms where most of their revenue is from overseas.

b. See Doug Casey's; hardassetsalliance.com, Caseyresearch.com , and internationalman.com.

c. The Dollar Vigilante: CEO Jeff Berwick started with a newsletter and TDV has grown to a family of services to guide investors into asset, and national diversification (i.e., foreign jurisdictions; visit; dollarvigilante.com). They offer services to create a Multi-Generational Succession Plan.

d. Thun Financial Advisors (ThunFinancial.com), is based in Madison, WI. Thun offers services for both foreign and USA residents, and buys assets from both.

e, The Sovereign Society (Sovereign-Society.com) offers services, and a book 'Where to Stash Your Cash Legally', by Robert Bauman JD. Also see Sovereign Offshore Services LLC.

f. WindRock Wealth Management (windrockwealth.com) uses free-market thinking to advise clients in today's world of significant government intervention in our economy.

g. Ron Holland and Frank Suess run Swiss firms bfi-consulting.com, bfi-capital.com, and bfi-wealth.com, which advise on choices outside the USD and USA. Global Gold Inc. (globalgold.ch) is a subsidiary of BFI Capital Group Inc. (www.bficapital.com). Claudio Grass is Managing Director at Global Gold AG, claudio.grass@globalgold.ch. Their newsletter is the Mountain Vision Update, at www.mountainvision.com.

h. Sprott Asset Management LP (www.sprott.com) is an alternative asset manager that offers a variety of investments including fully-allocated (your name is tied to certain coins or bars) gold and silver 'Physical Trusts'.

i. Fisher Investments (www.fisherinvestments.com) is one of the largest independent investment advisers. Ken Fisher, CEO, says; 'I hate annuities, and so should you!'

j. Grant's Interest Rate Observer (GrantsPub.com), edited by James Grant, is an independent, value-oriented and contrary-minded journal of the financial markets.

k. Weiss Research (weissinc.com, and weissresearchissues.com).

l. Trends Research.com, led by Gerald Celente. While not a financial advisor firm, they offer economic and other trends info that can help investors.

m. Other: There are a variety of 'traditional' sources at; cnnmoney.com/expert. See '101 Ways to Build Wealth' at: http://money.cnn.com/magazines/moneymag/101-ways-build-wealth/. Also look at   marketwatch.com , newworldinvestor.com, and theprudentspeculator.com. Search the Internet for 'Barrons 40 Largest'.

7. Diversification :

Until about year 2000, 'diversity' meant to avoid having too much of your investments in one industry, or type of security, or asset. Because of the U.S. and world economic chaos, that definition now includes foreign currency and foreign legal structures (jurisdictions) to minimize taxation and controls (ie, 'internationalization'). See FATCA on p. 86. Know the politics (corruption, restrictions, etc.) of the nations whose securities, private business stocks, land, and currency you buy, or use for storage. Note that negative trade balances and high debt-to-GDP ratio are a warning of likely future economic decline. The goal is to internationalize your assets in a tax efficient manner without losing control.

THE SOLUTION
Now that you are more aware of the worsening legal and currency investment risks you face, what should you do? The solution is to get your money out of the USD and invested in hard assets (farm land, real estate, firms that own hard assets (railroads, etc.), precious metals, etc.), or a foreign trust.(more on P.3-5, 80).

Closing Comment: I hope that what you have learned in this book will allow you to develop an investment plan that will help bring you more wealth, with less risk and taxation. I wish you Good and Safer Investing ! Please send comments to Redickd@aol.com. To see my essays on this, and other topics, go to my archive at ActivistPost.com, and select 'Contributors' at top of Home page, then my name.

Thanks for your interest. Let's work together, Dave Redick

Notes

Notes

Part 2: General Appendix

**Sections; 1. Info Sources, p. 88, 2. Articles, p.89,
 3. Glossary, p. 99, 4. Dave's Bio, p. 110.**

Section 1. Info Sources
A. Organizations:
Free-market and limited-government oriented essays, books, blogs, meetings, and courses.
1. The Cato Institute: www.cato.org
2. The Independent Institute: www.independent.org
3. The Ludwig von Mises Institute: Daily essays are at www.LewRockwell.com, plus books and articles at mises.org.
4. Reason Foundation: A magazine and www.reason.org
5. Foundation for Economic Education: www.Fee.org
B. Internet Sites:
1. For more on money and gold: visit en.wikipedia.org/wiki/Money_supply, https://en.wikipedia.org/wiki/Gold, fgmr.com, soundmoneydefense.org, gold.org, Mises.org, DollarCollapse.com, goldmoney.com, cmre.org, en.wikipedia.org/wiki/History_of_money, goldismoney.info, pgpf.org, measuringworth.com, MoneyWatch.com, transaction.net/money/lets/, xat.org/xat/moneyhistory, 321Gold.com, GATA.org, Kitco.com,

2. General Web Sites about Government & Economics:
See a flow of essays from; PaulCraigRoberts.org, LewRockwell.com, Activistpost.com, Antiwar.com, FFF.org, AmericansforProsperity.org, VDare.com, reason.org, pacificreasearch.org, freedomforceinternational.org, independent.org, pacificlegal.org, online.barrons.com, garynorth.com, dailyreckoning.com, pgpf.org, mises.org, shadowstats.com, economicpolicyjournal.com,

zerohedge.com, informationclearinghouse.info, TheBurningPlatform.com, trendsresearch.com, freedomworks.com, campaignforliberty.org, USDebtClock.org , the economiccollapseblog.com, economiccollapsenews.com, (dollarvigilante.com, tdvoffshore.com, tdvwealthmanagement.com, tdvpassports.com), Dave's essays, App. B, p.89.

Section 2. Articles:

****

Part A:

A1: The Top 5 Reasons Why You Should Get Out Of The Western Financial System Now

http://dollarvigilante.com/blog/2014/1/7/the-top-5-reasons-why-you-should-get-your-assets-out-of-the-.html

By; Jeff Berwick, Chief Editor,   dollarvigilante.com
                                    Jan. 7, 2014

Many people are not aware of the incredibly dire, impending risks of holding your assets in the Western world in the immediate future. Mainstream media will not tell you about much of this. Politicians and government definitely won't.

But, this is all factual information, all from government sources, in fact, with references that paints a very clear, dire picture. The picture couldn't really be any clearer once you see this information.

Here is just the top five of literally dozens of reasons why you should be looking to secure your assets now.

1. The International Monetary Fund (IMF) announced in Oct-2013 that due to government debt levels in developed (read: Western) countries being at 200 year highs that there will be severe "financial repression" necessary. What do they define as severe "financial repression"? They give a number of possibilities including outright debt default (which will cause a financial system collapse) or an "inflationary surprise" (hyperinflation, destroying the Western currencies). In either case, having your assets in a bank or brokerage account in the West will likely lead to near destruction of the value of your money/capital.

2. FATCA (Foreign Account Tax Compliance Act). Not many Americans know anything about this but if you do have money or assets outside of the US, you already are supposed to file a FBAR (which essentially means, 'tell us where your money is') and a Form 8389 (which essentially means, 'tell us where your assets are'). Failure to file is punishable by extreme fines. To make matters worse, if you don't have any assets or money outside of the US, FATCA is came into effect on July 1, 2014 and will all but end expatriation of your assets. (more at p. 88)

3. Worldwide Income Tax. Until just a few years ago it was only the US and Eritrea that actually demanded that you pay a worldwide income tax in your "home" country no matter where you lived or resided and no matter where you made your money. That is all changing fast. In just the last few years numerous countries including Australia, Mexico, Chile and others have all started to claim that even if you

90

are a non-resident citizen making money outside of the country you still owe tax to the country of your citizenship. In fact, as we will likely write about tomorrow, Panama just tried to enact a worldwide income tax over Christmas of this year. What this means is that if you don't structure your financial affairs properly it is quite likely that no matter where you live and what you do that you will owe a very significant percentage of your income to the countries (plural) in which you hold citizenship.

4. Bank Bail-Ins. You likely remember in the spring of 2013 the country of Cyprus just took nearly 50% of everyone's money in their bank account if they had more than $100,000 in their account. In effect, the opposite of something like the Federal Deposit Insurance Corporation (FDIC) where instead of protecting your funds the government just takes it. Many countries have since instituted "bank bail-in" clauses in laws which state that if banks have problems and need funds (which they will, see point **1.** above) that they are legally allowed to take their depositor's money. These places include every country in Europe, Canada, Australia and even the US. Jim Sinclair, chairman and chief executive officer of Tanzania Royalty Exploration Corp., and whose family started Goldman Sachs, Salomon Brothers, Lehman Brothers, and others, has been warning of this for a while. *"Bail-ins are coming to North America without any doubt....It stands on legal grounds by legal precedent both in the US, Canada and the UK,"* said Sinclair. (Insert; Sure enough, at the Nov-2014 annual G20 meeting, they agreed that all members would approve bail-is!)

5. Pension Fund Seizure. Think it can't happen? It has already happened in numerous countries and the US Treasury has discussed nationalizing all private pensions in the US. In 2009, Ireland seized €4 billion from its Pension Reserve fund. In 2010 Hungary told its citizens to remit their private pension funds to the government. Later in 2010 the French parliament took €33 billion from their national reserve pension fund and in 2011 $80 million in private retirement funds were transferred to the state's pension scheme in Bulgaria. And, in September of 2013 the Polish government confiscated the bulk of the assets of the country's private pension funds. The writing on the wall is clear, they will also come for your pensions... and that is beyond the Social Security funds that have already long been taken and spent.

...if those five reasons alone don't have you incredibly concerned about salvaging your wealth then there is probably nothing more I can do to help you. None of the above five reasons for the need to do so are conjecture. They all come direct from the IMF and the US government who have announced their intentions. It can't get any clearer than that. *(Jeff Berwick is the founder of The Dollar Vigilante, CEO of TDV Media & Services and host of a popular video podcast.)*

More: The links below add to Appendix A:

A2: http://dollarvigilante.com/blog/2014/1/6/the-imf-just-announced-they-will-take-all-your-money-and-you.html

The IMF Just Announced They Will Take All Your Money and You Won't Believe How Obviously They Did It! By Jeff Berwick, dollarvigilante.com, Jan. 6, 2014

A3: http://dollarvigilante.com/blog/2012/6/21/fbar-8398-fatca-and-capital-controls-the-trail-that-leads-to.htm.
FBAR, 8398, FATCA, and Capital Controls - The Trail That Leads to the Forced Repatriation of Your Foreign Assets. By, Jim Karger, TDV Legal Correspondent, www.DollarVigilante.com , June-2012

Part B: Links to Dave's Published Essays

Note: For convenience, you can go to ActivistPost.com, select 'Contributors' at the top of the Home page, and, then my name. There you can click on any of the links below, rather than typing them out.

B1- Economics and Personal Investment

1) How is Independent Thinking is Connected to Freedom and Prosperity, Aug-2010 ; Explores the concept of Independent Thinking, where a person decides what to believe and do, rather than seeking the comfort of following the mainstream. http://www.activistpost.com/2010/08/how-is-independent-thinking-connected.html

2) New Factors in Personal Finance Jan-2013; Today's world has financial risks that have never existed before, so much of the 'traditional' planning logic is wrong or has voids. http://www.activistpost.com/2013/07/new-factors-in-personal-financial.html#more

3) Internationalize to Protect and Grow Your Assets; 20Jan2014; This article is designed for investors who are willing consider the added diversification of 'Internationalization' by converting most of their assets into trusts, and safer foreign currencies and nations.

http://www.activistpost.com/2014/01/internationalize-to-protect-and-grow.html

B2 - Monetary Systems

1) Why Use Gold as Money? , Dec-2010 ; The benefits of using a commodity as money, and why the market prefers gold.

http://www.activistpost.com/2010/12/why-use-gold-as-money.html

2) How to Abolish the Fed and Convert to Gold as Money , Jan-2011; A five-step plan to convert the US to gold as money, allow private mints, and the benefits it would bring.

http://www.activistpost.com/2011/01/how-to-abolish-fed-and-convert-to-gold.html#

3) The Impact of Fiat Money as the World's Reserve Currency , Aug-2010; As issuer of the world's primary reserve currency, the USA can create new money to pay its' bills. Since ending the Dollar's gold 'backing' in 1971 (thus 'fiat'), the USA has created $trillions of new money and the dollar value has declined by about 80%.
http://www.activistpost.com/2010/09/impact-of-fiat-money-as-worlds-reserve.html#more

4) A Plan to Save the Euro with Gold'   Nov. 30, 2011

European 'leaders' are in a panic to save the Euro! I offer a plan that could be invoked by Euro issuing nations with no risk to current Euro owners because all existing Euro currency would immediately be backed by gold.
http://www.activistpost.com/2011/11/three-step-plan-to-save-euro-with-gold.html#more

5) 'Convert the USA Monetary System to Gold'
Jan. 25, 2012; This essay shows a detailed plan to implement conversion from fake Fed Notes to 'gold-as-money' (all free market, with private mints, no Fed, redeemable paper notes, gold weight as the unit of account, etc.
http://www.activistpost.com/2012/01/convert-usa-monetary-system-to-gold.html#more

6) 'Germany Should Quit the Euro and Use Gold As Money', Sep. 1, 2012; The fiat Euro (no gold 'backing') gave politicians and banks a way to create new money to feed excess spending and debt. Germany has the strength to lead the Euro Zone to gold as money.
http://www.activistpost.com/2012/09/germany-should-quit-euro-and-use-gold.html#more

7) The Key Factors in a Sustainable Gold Standard for Money, Aug. 30, 2014; In this article I review basic issues and comment on some of the recently proposed plans.
http://www.activistpost.com/2014/08/the-key-factors-in-sustainable-gold.html#more

B3- Government Structure and Conduct

1) The Phases of Empires , Aug-2010 ; How empires rise and fall, and how five key characteristics vary.

http://www.activistpost.com/2010/08/phases-of-empire.html#more

2) The Cost of Building and Operating Empire-USA ,
 Aug-2010; How owning colonies/territories, or controlling other countries, damages the economics, civil rights, and morals of the Homeland.

http://www.activistpost.com/2010/08/cost-of-building-and-operating-empire.html#more

3) How Excess Spending, Taxation, and Controls are Destroying the US Economy , Jan-2011; How excess spending, taxation, and controls by government for wars, welfare, entitlements, subsidies, etc., mostly financed by debt or fake money from our central bank, is wrecking our economy and morals.

http://www.activistpost.com/2011/01/how-excess-spending-taxation-and.html

4) Should Government Manage the Economy? ,

March 15, 2011; The biggest divides in thinking as to the proper role of government are whether it should; 1. Manage the economy, 2. Be paternalistic (education, health, pensions, etc., or 3. Just protect the rights of its citizens (ie, comply with the constitution). http://www.activistpost.com/2011/03/should-government-manage-economy.html#more

5) 'Save the USA by Restoring Government to its proper Role' , Nov. 2, 2012 ; USA governments at all levels (city, county, state, federal) are causing great social and economic harm with their regulations, spending, and abuses.http://www.activistpost.com/2011/04/save-usa-by-restoring-government-to-its.html#more

6) Economic and Cultural Decay in the USA; Jan. 11, 2014; The USA is in the failure phase of Empire-USA. All empires fail due to excessive spending for wars and welfare. Sadly, the USA is a classic example! http://www.activistpost.com/2014/07/economic-and-cultural-decay-in-usa.html

7) 'Why the USA is Losing Power, Jobs, and Respect, but Making Enemies', Oct. 28, 2014; The USA has been an aggressive empire, seeking more political and economic powers since the 'War of 1812'. We are now a failing Empire. http://www.activistpost.com/2014/10/why-usa-is-losing-power-jobs-and.html
xxxxxx

Part C: Table 6: Weight: Conversion
Common units for precious metals.

1 Tonne (metric) = 2,205 pounds (Lbs) = 1,000 Kilograms (Kg)
$$= 32,150 \text{ troy oz.}$$
1 US Ton (Short) = 2,000 Lbs advp.   =   907.2 Kg
1 UK Ton (Long) = 2,240 Lbs advp.   = 1,016.5 Kg
1 gram   = 15.43 grains = 5 metric carats = 0.643 pennyweight
1 Troy Ounce = 31.10 grams = 480 grains (gr)= 120 engl. carats
1 Troy Pound   = 12 Troy ounces (Oz) = 373.2 grams
1 Avoirdupois Lb= 16 avp. ounces= 453.6 grams=7,000 grains
1 Avp. ounce   = 28.35 grams (g), 437.5 grains
1 English carat   = 1.296 metric carats (for precious stones)

% Gold	Europe System	Carat System (see next page)
	Fineness	
100.0	1.000	24 carat
91.7	0.917	22
75.0	0.750	18
58.5	0.585	14
41.6	0.416	10 (see next page)

(see Notes below)

Notes for Table 6:
1. The 'Long Ton' is the Imperial system used in the UK
2. The 'Short Ton' is used in the US and Canada.
3. The IMF and all nations measure their gold in metric tonnes.
4. Gold weighs 19,320 kg per cubic meter. Tungsten is close at 19,600, so it is sometimes gold plated and used as fake gold bars and ingots. Steel is 7,850, copper 8,930, lead 11,340, and water 1,000.
5. Grains, grams, and Tonne are metric units. The Troy system was started by King Henry II of England. The Avoirdupois system evolved through common usage in Europe.
6. Fineness: The purity of a precious metal measured in 1,000 parts of an alloy: a gold bar of 0.995 fineness contains 995 parts gold and 5 parts of another metal; a 0.999 coin is 99.9% pure.

Section 3: Glossary:

1. Appreciation: An increase in value, such as increased purchasing power of money. Opposite of 'depreciation'.

2. Central Bank: Whether private or owned by the government, a central bank usually has certain government-bestowed duties and privileges such as; a) The sole right to issue currency and market government securities, b) Allowed to operate in almost total secrecy to supposedly avoid political influence, c) Set national interest rates, d) Buy government securities to fund government expenses, e) Stabilize the value of the currency and keep unemployment low (these may be fake duties, as with the U.S. Fed, but sound good!), f) Serves as the 'Lender of Last Resort' to banks short of cash (a sweet deal for casino bankers!), and g) other acts. The CB managers typically work closely with their government leaders (thus politicized), and key managers may be appointed by the government. In the U.S., it is the Federal Reserve System. **Dave says this about central banks; 1) They do far more harm than good (constant, often politicized, meddling instead of free-market clearing of problems), and 2) All were created by and for politicians and bankers so they never run out of money!**

3. COMEX: Formerly **'The Commodity Exchange, Inc.'**, is now a metals exchange in the CME Group (cmegroup.com), which also owns 'The New York Mercantile Exchange' (NYMEX). The other two designated contract markets in the CME Group are the Chicago Mercantile Exchange (CME) and the Chicago Board of Trade (CBOT). COMEX is a primary market for trading metals such as gold, silver, copper and aluminum. Combined with NYMEX, they are the world's largest physical metals futures trading exchange.

4. Commodities: For 'goods' (not 'services'), a commodity is substance that can be described as a standard (type, grade, etc.) and thus be considered the same substance in any market. Location doesn't matter, except for delivery cost. Generally, these are basic resources and agricultural products such as iron ore, crude oil, coal, salt, sugar, tea, coffee beans, soybeans, tobacco, aluminum, copper, rice, wheat, and precious metals. Soft commodities are goods that are grown, while hard commodities are the ones that are extracted through mining. Well-established physical commodities have actively traded spot and derivative markets. Some commodities have been used as money (see P. 54).

5. Contrarian Investor; One who profits by investing against the conventional wisdom. Opposite of the Lemmings or Sheep, that prefer to be viewed as 'normal and safe' and follow the crowd despite warning signs.

6. Deflation: The opposite of Monetary Inflation; a reduction in the money supply as a % of GDP, and an increase in purchasing power of each money unit, thus lower prices. Not to be confused with 'depression' or 'depreciation'.

7. Depression: Any economic downturn where real GDP (Gross Domestic product) declines by more than 10 percent. Also; Two or more quarters of reduced GDP. A **recession** is an economic downturn that is less severe.

8. Economic Systems: (Types, alpha order)

a. 'Austrian School' of economic thought (Hayek, von Mises, Rothbard), emphasizes the spontaneous organizing power of free market pricing, decisions by individuals, gold as money, and little or no government management or stimulation of the economy.

b. Capitalism - An 'economic system' based on private ownership, free enterprise, and minimal regulation. It offers more than economic results. **It is a moral system** that depends on willing buyers and sellers within the rule of law, not coercion and control by others. It has been re-defined as a mean, self-centered, you're on your own, 'social system' by those who prefer Socialism (sharing by force, causing a more equal but lower te gold of living for all). **The U.S. now has 'Crony Capitalism'**, a damaging distortion where firms get favors from government (often in exchange for campaign donations!). It creates privilege for the few at the expense of the many.

c. Communism: The government owns all housing, agriculture, industry and transportation (almost everything but the clothes on your back). The government tells you where to live, go to college (if any), and where to work.

d. Fascism allows private ownership of businesses, but there is extensive government control and preeminence.

e. 'Keynesian Theory' (started by J. M. Keynes and now used by Krugman, Samuelson, Stiglitz, Bernanke, and Yellen) depends on massive use of government fiscal (spending) and monetary (interest rates, money supply) policy trying to create prosperity or avoid and end depressions. History and logic show the Keynes approach is unsustainable and never works for more than a year or two (longer if supported by natural resources; oil, timber, mining, etc.).

f. Monetarism: An approach identified with the 'Chicago School of economics led by Prof. Milton Friedman Ph.D. of the University of Chicago. It emphasizes management of the money supply by the Fed to control inflation and GDP growth. Most Monetarists dislike the gold standard as 'too inflexible' in changing the money supply, except by mining more gold or silver. They are wrong because they ignore how the purchasing power of gold increases with more demand. Thus, there is always 'enough'.

g. Socialism: Most of the means of production and trade (factories, railroads, etc) are owned by the government, which sets pricing, product types, etc. The government controls most wages, with an emphasis on 'fairness', need, and 'hours worked', rather than value of the service performed. High, and steeply progressive, taxes support a 'single-payer health system and pension plan

h. 'Supply Side' economics: This school of thought emphasizes incentive to invest by reductions in; **a.** capital gains and income taxes, and **b.** regulation. These should be the first steps to revive a troubled economy because they have the lasting effect of stimulating action by producers and investors. "Supply Side' was originated by economists P. C. Roberts Ph.D., Robert Mundell Ph.D., and Arthur Laffer Ph.D., and politicians Pres. Ronald Reagan and Rep. Jack Kemp in the 1980s.

9. Fiat Money: Fiat ('by decree') money is worth whatever the government says it is (face value), although the material of which it is made may have more or less market value (examples; one ounce silver dollars and worthless paper, both declared worth $1; one ounce American Eagle gold coin with face value of $50).

10. Fiscal Policy: Management of government spending to fulfill obligations, and in some cases to 'stimulate', or 'guide', the economy.

11. Free Market: A market that is free from government intervention (i.e., regulation, subsidies, price controls, or governmental monopolies, etc.). In a free market, property rights (ownership of goods and services) are voluntarily exchanged at a price and terms arranged solely by the mutual consent of sellers and buyers/consumers, with no government control of pricing, creation of new firms, pay and benefits, hiring and firing, etc.

12. Gang Theft: This occurs when one group of people in some manner overpowers another group, and forcibly takes assets from them. Most people agree that it is immoral, and should be illegal, but oddly, most people believe it is OK to employ gang-theft-by-vote to tax, restrict, or control others (usually 'the rich'), via government power as the larger group sees fit. They justify it by making their victims pay their 'fair share', or 'they got rich by luck', etc. **This in fact describes an immoral government and a 'penalty on success',** thus a reverse incentive.

13. Gross Domestic Product (GDP): The market value of all final goods and services made within the borders of a country in a year. **Gross National Product (GNP)** is GDP plus income received from other countries (interest and dividends), less similar payments made to other countries.

14. Inflation: a. Monetary Inflation: A rapid and excessive expansion of the money supply (such as over 5% per year; more than growth of GNP); purchasing power of a given monetary unit (Dollar, etc.) is reduced, **b. Price Inflation:** Increase in current prices due to reduced purchasing power of the money usually caused by an excessive increase in the money supply (or other factors such as reduced supply, increased demand, cartel pricing, etc.). The 'Nominal' price is the 'listed', or 'current' price. The 'Real' price is a past or future nominal price adjusted for price inflation. 'Hyper' inflation is a rapid and continuing increase of prices (over 50 %/mo.), the supply of money, and the cost of goods.

15. International Monetary Fund (IMF):
The International Monetary Fund is an international organization, headquartered in Washington, DC, of 188 countries working to foster global monetary cooperation, secure financial stability, facilitate international trade, promote high employment and sustainable economic growth, and reduce poverty around the world. Sounds nice,

but in fact the funds from most loans to nations is used to pay other bank loans, and the people must pay the IMF. The Banksters win again! It was formed in 1944 as part of the Bretton Woods Agreement. (see SDR, #22 below), as was the World Bank. (#26).

16. Internationalize: This is the process done by investors who are concerned about decline of their domestic currency values, and increased taxes, capital controls, and confiscation. At a minimum, they convert their assets to denomination in a stronger foreign currency in an 'investor friendly' country, but this does not help minimize U.S. taxes, etc. A more complete approach is to work with a professional (lawyer, accountant, Wealth Management Financial Advisor) to set up an International Business Company (or Limited Liability Corporation), a tax minimization trust, and banking, in one or more foreign jurisdictions (nations).

17. Mercantilism: An system where the ruling government seeks wealth, especially gold or silver bullion, by playing a protectionist role in the economy, and by encouraging exports and discouraging imports, notably through the use of import tariffs, subsidies to domestic firms, and money valuation. The opposite is a policy of laissez-faire, which says that all trade is good and that such controls are counterproductive, and usually evolve to be used as political favors.

18. Monetary Policy: Management of the monetary system; money supply, bank reserves, interest rates, etc.

19. Money: (mostly from wikipedia.org) Money is anything that is generally accepted as payment for goods and services and repayment of debts. The main functions of money are distinguished as: a medium of exchange, a unit of account, and a store and measure of value.

Money originated as **commodity money,** then evolved to easier-to-transport representative money in which a paper certificate, or base-metal coin can be redeemed by the Bearer on demand to the Issuer (Mint). However, nearly all contemporary money systems at the national level are fiat money systems. **Fiat money** is without value as a physical commodity, and derives its value by being declared by a government to be **legal tender**; that is, it must be accepted when offered, and at face value (USD, Euro, etc.). See P. 38 for M-0,1, 2, 3.

20. Principle: An underlying guide to thinking and action. A comprehensive and fundamental law, doctrine, or assumption. A rule or code of conduct.

21. Reserves: 1. Fractional Reserve Banking today means the bank need only retain a certain percent of deposits on hand (typically about ten percent) and can loan the rest. In fact, this means banks can loan up to ten times the amount of their deposits, thereby creating new money! For example, a $1,000 deposit can be the reserve for $10,000 of new loans. **2. 'Reserve Currency'** is the money of a certain nation that by agreement or common usage; 1. can be used by banks as their 'reserve' ('good as gold') which underpins their loans and obligations, and 2. is acceptable for payments between other countries worldwide.

22. Special Drawing Rights (SDR): Special drawing rights (XDR or SDR) are supplementary foreign exchange reserve assets defined and maintained by the International Monetary Fund (IMF). Their value is based on a basket of key international currencies reviewed by IMF every five years. Based on the latest review conducted on December 30, 2010, the XDR basket consists of the following four currencies: U.S. dollars ($) 41.9 % , euro (€) 37.4 %, pounds sterling (£) 11.3 %, and the Japanese yen (¥) 9.4 %.The weights assigned to each currency in the XDR basket are adjusted to take into account their current prominence in terms of international trade and national foreign exchange reserves.

The XDR is not a currency per se. They instead represent a claim to currency held by IMF member countries for which they may be exchanged. As they can only be exchanged for U.S. dollars ($), euro (€), pounds sterling (£), or Japanese yen (¥), XDRs may actually represent a potential claim on IMF member countries' non-gold foreign exchange reserves, which are usually held in those currencies. Being the unit of account for the IMF has long been the main function of the XDR.[5]

 Special Drawing Rights are denoted with the ISO 4217 currency code XDR. XDRs are allocated to countries by the IMF. Private parties do not hold or use them.

(https://en.wikipedia.org/wiki/Special_drawing_rights)

23. Standards for Gold-Based Monetary Systems

The gold standard is a monetary system in which the unit of account is weight of gold. Prices are by weight and purity.

1) The **Gold Specie Standard** is the system in which the monetary unit is associated with a circulating gold coin. (paper notes, if any, have 100% reserves for redeemability)

2) The **Gold Exchange Standard** may involve only the circulation of silver coins, or coins made of other metals, but the authorities will have guaranteed a fixed exchange rate with another country that is on the gold standard, hence creating a *de facto* gold standard. An example is the Bretton Woods Agreement of 1944.

3) The **Gold Bullion Standard** is a system in which gold coins do not actually circulate, but in which the authorities have agreed to sell gold bullion on demand at a fixed price.

(from http://en.wikipedia.org/wiki/Gold_standard)

4) The **Private Gold Standard;** Under this plan, money is produced by private firms in the free market where customers (users of money) decide which type and source of money they prefer, and mints compete for customers. There is no central bank (our Fed), and government mints (run by the Treasury), if any, are optional, and have no control or privilege over the private mints.
The free market is allowed to work! The 'unit of account', and thus pricing, is **weight** of the commodity (typically gold and silver) used as money. The gold may be alloyed for hardness, etc., but only the amount of pure 24 carat gold would count. Mints would be required to hold 100% gold reserves for redemption of paper notes and base-metal coins. Banks could hold fractional-reserves for savings deposits, but would be required to disclose the fraction to depositors.

24. SWIFT: The **Society for Worldwide Interbank Financial Telecommunication** (**SWIFT**) provides a network that enables financial institutions worldwide **to send and receive information** about financial transactions (but not 'execute' them) in a secure, standardized and reliable environment. The majority of international interbank messages use the SWIFT network. As of September 2010, SWIFT linked more than 9,000 financial institutions in 209 countries and territories. SWIFT is a cooperative society under Belgian law owned by its member financial institutions with offices around the world. The USA has major influence over it's services

25. US Dollar Index (USDX): It is a measure of the value of the United States dollar relative to a basket of foreign currencies. It is a **weighted geometric mean** of the dollar's value compared only with "basket" of 6 other major currencies which are, '% by weight': Euro (EUR), 57.6%, Japanese yen (JPY) 13.6%, Pound sterling (GBP), 11.9%, Canadian dollar (CAD), 9.1%, Swedish krona (SEK), 4.2%, and Swiss franc (CHF) 3.6% .

More at; http://en.wikipedia.org/wiki/U.S._Dollar_Index)

26. World Bank: The **World Bank** was formed in 1944 as part of the Bretton Woods Agreement. It is an international financial institution that provides loans to developing countries for capital programs. It comprises two institutions: the International Bank for Reconstruction and Development (IBRD) and the International Development Association (IDA). The World Bank is a component of the **World Bank Group**, and a member of the United Nations Development Group. The World Bank's official goal is the reduction of poverty. According to its Articles of Agreement, all its decisions must be guided by a commitment to the promotion of foreign investment and international trade and to the facilitation of capital investment (see IMF, 14 above)

27.. World Gold Council: The WGC (Gold.org), based in London, UK, with operations in India, the Far East and the USA, the World Gold Council is an association whose members comprise the world's leading gold mining companies. The WGC aims to maximize the industry's potential growth by monitoring and defending existing gold consumption. It also co-sponsors research in the development of new uses of gold, or of new products containing gold. For example, successful projects supported by the gold industry have led to the development of jewelry containing 99% gold. The WGC was also the creator of the first gold ETF.

As of September, 2017, WGC has these 18 members: Acacia, Agnico Eagle, Alamos Gold Inc., Barrick, Buenaventura, Centerra Gold, China Gold, Eldorado Gold,

Franco-Nevada, Goldcorp, Golden Star Resources, Kinross Gold, New Gold, Newmont, Primero, Royal Gold, Silver Wheaton, and Yamana Gold.

Section 4. Biography of Dave Redick

Personal: Dave was born in 1935 and grew up with his two brothers in a middle class family near Detroit, MI. When he was 14, the family moved to an 80-acre general farm near Ann Arbor, Michigan. He has an honorable discharge from the U.S. Army Reserve. After 46 years in California, he moved to Madison, WI in 2004.

Education and Business: Dave won a four-year tuition scholarship to the University of Michigan, based on grades, activities (Sr. Class President, sports), and need, and started in the September, 1953. He completed his **BS-Engineering** in 1958, and passed the academic exams for the Michigan Society of Professional Engineers (EIT). He first worked as an aerospace engineer for 5 years (rocket engines and satellites) in California, and then started his career in telecom sales and management. In 1965 he earned an **MBA** with an **Economics** major from Santa Clara University in Santa Clara, CA. After management positions in several other firms, in 1995 he became **VP Sales, then President**, of a wireless telecom consulting engineering firm www.hntelecom.com. He left in 2000 to be **VP and cofounder** of a Silicon Valley telecom startup 'Fiberstreet' (closed, see Google), and **helped raise $6 million of venture capital**.

Since 2009 he has worked as a Speaker, and Author of books, on the interaction of governments, business, people, and economics, with a focus on Monetary Systems and Wealth Management. His views are shown in this book, and other books on Amazon.com,

** End of Book **

www.ingramcontent.com/pod-product-compliance
Lightning Source LLC
Chambersburg PA
CBHW051811170526
45167CB00005B/1974